A Ceremony
for Every Occasion

The Wheel of the Year
and Rites of Passage

A Ceremony
for Every Occasion

The Wheel of the Year
and Rites of Passage

Siusaidh Ceanadach

Winchester, UK
Washington, USA

First published by Moon Books, 2012
Moon Books is an imprint of John Hunt Publishing Ltd., Laurel House, Station Approach,
Alresford, Hants, SO24 9JH, UK
office1@o-books.net
www.o-books.com

For distributor details and how to order please visit the 'Ordering' section on our website.

Text copyright: Siusaidh Ceanadach 2011

ISBN: 978 1 84694 841 1

A CIP catalogue record for this book is available from the British Library.

Design: Stuart Davies
Cover design and line drawings: Nina Falaise

Printed and bound by CPI Group (UK) Ltd., Croydon, CR0 4YY
Printed in the USA by Offset Paperback Mfrs, Inc

We operate a distinctive and ethical publishing philosophy in all
areas of our business, from our global network of authors to
production and worldwide distribution.

CONTENTS

Midwinter Solstice and Yule

Acknowledgements

Before you start to read and use this book I must tell you that a few of the calls in some of the ceremonies have been written by members of Tuatha De Bridget, the Druidcraft Open Group that I co-organise with my partner and husband Piet, and also with our daughter Pauline here in Glasgow, Scotland. Where there are large areas of a ceremony that have been written by anyone else, other than me I have said so at the end of the chapter.

I would like to thank all the members of Tuatha De Bridget, both past and present for their permission to use these calls, I am very grateful as it allows the flow of the rituals.

I would also like to say how happy I am that Nina Falaise*, who is a visionary artist, agreed to use her gifts to create a cover design and also line drawings within the book.

I must also thank Glasgow City Council Land Services Department for their continued support and help in allowing our group to use the Ancient Earthworks in Pollok Country Park. Without their help in the first place, none of these ceremonies would have been possible and I would never have had the material to write about.

And I just have to say a great big thank you to our distant cousin Maria who has done such a lot in encouraging me to write, and for all the help she has given me over the last year.

*Nina Falaise was born in Skipton, Yorkshire.

Nina has been an active participant in the Western Mystery tradition for many years, contributing her experience of dance, mask making and choreography to ceremonial rituals. Nina is a Visionary artist, who's art is inspired through ritual, meditation and her on going studies of the Great Work. Nina has illustrated for several books, including Daughters of Danu by Piet Ceanadach and What Brave Bulls Do by Rohase Piercy. For artwork commissions by Nina, contact: nina.falaise@yahoo.com

Introduction

For the last few years, I have been writing rituals, helping run them and generally organize these with the help of my partner and husband. It started when we moved up to Glasgow in 2001 and when my daughter was running a Druid Grove, Caer Clud, with a friend of hers, we went along to support her, whilst at the same time continuing to practice our own spiritual path, that of Wiccan. Gradually the Druid folk either moved away, went on to other things or just chose to practice as solitaries, and during that time we took over running the four cross quarter fire festivals, Imbolc, Beltane, Lughnasadh and Samhain. Then came the day when it was decided that the Druid Grove would go into 'sleep' mode and cease to hold ceremonies.

At this point, we had to do some very serious thinking, did we want to take on all eight festivals and if so what changes should there be? We made the step and *Tuatha De Bridget took over all major festivals of the Wheel of the Year and we further more opened these up to anyone in the Pagan Community and anyone of 'good heart'.

Since then our numbers have gradually risen and we are supported by Glasgow City Council's Land Services department and have official permission to hold all these ceremonies.

Much of this time Piet, my husband and working partner had been writing a book, due to be published this year, 2011. Then a distant cousin, a clanswomen of Piet's Irish Clan suggested I put all this together and write a book about the festivals, giving rituals, lists and information on how to celebrate the turning of 'The Wheel of the Year' and this little book was born.

I wanted to give everyone the opportunity to read and use these rituals, to perhaps use them as a template to help their own group, or simply as a teaching aid to getting to know our Pagan Path. These can be used as they are, can be adapted to include local

Deity, or can be used by a couple or a single person, with a little adjustment. All I ask is that if you do use these ceremonies that you acknowledge me as the writer on the cover, perhaps at the back. Most of the rituals are written by me. Where I have added words written by another member of the group, I have let you know this.

Although the Celtic Pagan year starts at Samhain, I have started at Imbolc, with the tiny snowdrops peeping up from the frozen land here in Scotland and the days still growing longer from the longest night and shortest day of Midwinter. There is always a gap in ceremonies and gatherings after Yule as folks just manage to get around in the depths of winter and have enough struggles in day-to-day life. With Spring on its way there are some bright frosty days and the Ewes become heavy with their lambs and start to come into milk ready for lambing.

Naturally lambing itself will take place at different times depending on how high you live above sea level and how cold it is getting overnight. Up in the Southern Uplands of Scotland this does not actually take place until April 1st, but at lower pastures it can be much earlier and in some places farmers will lamb indoors just after Yule in order to grow their lambs big enough to use as breeding Tups or Rams in the Autumn.

As the year goes on, we come to the Spring Equinox or Ostara, the latter from which comes the word 'Easter'. A time of balance, of equal day and equal night. At this time, we celebrate new growth, and are again reminded of the fertility with colored eggs and paintings of the Hare. We dye hardboiled eggs at this time, using food dye, just a simple thing or some very artistic folks paint them with all kinds of patterns. If you take a small white wax candle and draw a pattern onto the egg, then boil it in colored water you will find that where you have drawn with the wax, the color does not seep in and you have a very simple offering for your egg basket. You need to add a little bit of vinegar into the water for this to help 'set' the color, white spirit vinegar is best. This is something that all

2

the children also enjoy doing.

All our eggs are put into a basket at the start of the ceremony and are blessed, asking Spirit and Deity to bless each one and take that blessing to the person who chooses the egg. At the end of the ceremony, we share them all out and sometime add a few chocolate egg sized offerings so those who do not eat eggs can also have one.

If you have children or adults who can't eat either, then perhaps a nice idea is to get some empty egg shaped containers and put some wild flower seeds in them, then folk can take these and plant them in their garden or perhaps in a grassy area near them.

We progress onto Beltane and here the theme is on love, on fertility and on the joining of the Goddess to the God. We choose a 'May Queen' who in turn can choose a 'May King' and for those of a more Wiccan frame of mind this is our way of having a 'Maiden' and 'Stag'. During this ceremony, we will tie colored ribbons onto a simple headdress, which the May Queen wears. We may also tie the wrists of the couple, in the same manner we would in a Handfasting. We bring along a broomstick and get the couple to jump this and then offer this to anyone who wants to jump it also. We have in the past also made a maypole, woven it together with music and then tied this fast until Samhain. In this book you will find a ceremony for Beltane which features a May Queen and King.

The Wheel turns some more and we come to the Summer Solstice, when the day is at its longest and the night its shortest here in the UK. A great deal is written about Druids who go along to Stonehenge and watch for the rise of the Sun on its longest day and this is a wonderful sight, from what I have seen on the TV. Although the experts will tell you that Stonehenge was built in line with the Midwinter Solstice and the re-birth of the new sun.

The Male aspect of Divinity, the God is at his strongest, with powerful heat that is helping the corn and other grain in the fields to ripen, his power extends to all of life giving warmth, energy and lifting the spirits of all who live on this planet. Therefore, it is only natural that we celebrate his life, his power and the very important part he plays in our lives. The balance of the scales is tipped over towards the God and the Sun at this time of year and we need to find a man who can take on this role in our ceremony. We always have a call to both Female and Male Deity, but we need to remember here that the maturity of the person taking on this role. Now if you don't have anyone suitable to undertake this part then you will need someone with acting skills, someone who will take on this aspect for the festival, this could easily be done by a women and maybe someone with that inner strength that reflects the Sun's power.

On again we go to Lughnasadh and to the first of the Harvest Festivals, the Corn. We need a loaf of bread for this one, and maybe even a sheath of corn. We now have to remember that the God who we elevated in our midst at Midsummer is going to make a sacrifice; his golden corn is to be cut down in order to feed the people. In a way, he is going to give his life for the sake of his children. So this Harvest Festival is perhaps a bitter sweet one, giving great thanks for the life the Sun has given to the crops and acknowledge that in order for things to go on, we have to cut down this beautiful golden corn.

Now if you live in a city this may all sound very distant to you and maybe the Wheel of the Year does have another added bonus, it helps us all connect and think about where our food comes from, how its grown and what happens to it in order that we might go to the supermarket and buy our weekly groceries.

It's a very nice idea to make a simple bread plat for this ceremony and this is not nearly as difficult as it may seem. Buy a packet of bread mix and follow the instructions on the packet, once you have 'proved' the dough and it has risen the first time, roll it into a big fat sausage shape. Pinch one end together and with a sharp knife cut the remaining part of the dough into three, lengthways. Then moving each strand of dough into the middle over the centre piece, first one side and then the other, in a few moves you will have a braid. Pinch the other ends together, brush a mixture of egg and milk onto the shaped dough and leave it to 'rise' which would take around forty minutes, or however long it states on the packet. You need to bake this in a hot oven for the first ten minutes and then you can reduce the heat until the loaf is cooked. Leave it to cool when cooked and then you can take it along to your ceremony and share it amongst your friends, leaving some for the *Shee* the Faery Folk and for nature.

By the time we get to the Autumn Equinox the Harvest should be in full swing, all the other grain crops should have been gathered in and the berries are ready or getting ready to be picked. Still out in the farmlands the cattle are grazing on the green grass, the lambs have grown so large now that many of them are being separated from their mothers, either to grow on or for market. The warmth of the Sun is still helping to grow vegetables and berries. Another time of balance, of perhaps taking new steps, having grown in maturity and understanding you may wish to choose this time of the year for a Dedication to your Spiritual Path?

Alternatively, you may want to choose this festival as your group "Harvest Festival" and bring things to the ceremony that you can take along and share with others who may need them. If neither of these ideas appeals to you then at the very least celebrate the years turning and acknowledge the part that the farmers and growers of our food are playing in bringing nourishment to the people. How many folks know where their food comes from? Ask a child where his chips come from and he'll say 'Tesco's' or 'Asda' maybe 'Walmart' or some other food chain. Children don't stop and think about who grows the potatoes, digs them up, washes and cuts them. The majority will believe that you buy them in the shop and cook them. Or maybe you get them from MacDonald's!

So perhaps it's a very good time of the year to think about all of this and try and connect with the land and with Mother Earth. We can teach our little ones or those we have contact with more about the ever turning cycle of growth, harvest and the fallow period that it all needs for resting until it's time to plant the new seeds.

As the year slips around we come to one of the best known festivals of the year, Samhain (sow-een), it's that time of year when as Pagans we feel that the veil between this life and the otherworld is at its thinnest. It's a time of year for 'Remembrance', a time to pay some respect to those who have lived, died and moved on to what we call 'The Summerlands', the place of the ever young where the Sun is always shinning. We know that this is a different realm, one of spirit and not of body, but we need to paint a picture for the sake of others and the young. When someone we love dies, we feel such grief, but not necessarily for them, for us. We are going to miss these people, we can't hug them anymore, we can't call them up for a chat and we can't see them. Therefore, we need to celebrate their life, and show some respect for their achievements and this is the time of year we make a real point of this.

This whole time of year has been taken over with orange pumpkins, witches costumes, and trick and treating and I am not suggesting at all that any of this should be taken away from our little ones. However, we can bring this into our seasonal ceremony and make this a very colorful time. I do suggest that you read aloud the names of those who have passed from this life to the next in the last twelve months, and you read poems in their memory or sing songs or play music that you know they would like. We should also remember our ancestors who walked this earth before us. We in our group say, 'of line, blood and place'. It's the end of the Celtic Year and the start of the New Year so it's a mixture of happiness and sadness and time for some good mead.

Bring some berries along to your gatherings, but also bring a few sweeties for your young ones, encourage folks to wear robes to your meeting place, it's the one time of year that no one is likely to comment on seeing a gathering of 'Witches' and folks dressed in what will seem like fancy dress, so enjoy the freedom.

The Sun is now growing weaker and weaker as we come to the shortest day and the very longest night and our next celebration is the Midwinter Solstice with Yule just a few days after. Our ancestors have always celebrated at this time of the year, watching and waiting for the Sun, the new God to be re-born and to grow stronger three minutes a day from the Solstice.

I'm writing this in Scotland and its possible you may be on the other side of the world and this would be your Midsummer. If this is the case you need to switch the festivals around to match your own agricultural year and this can be done fairly easily. You can still use all the ceremonies but when they match the Wheel of the Year in your part of the World.

Here in Glasgow we meet early, on the actual date of our Midwinter ceremony, an hour earlier, this is two fold, to allow everyone to spend time with their family and to avoid anyone going home in the dark if they are alone.

We are watching at this time of the year for the birth of the new Divine Sun. The Goddess labors for hours through this longest night. None of us sure if this new Divine light has been reborn until we see for ourselves the length of the day starting to stretch out, which shows in about four days, just in time for Yule.

It is time for a great celebration with a special blend of incense and some mulled red wine or juice. We share seasonal cakes or pies during this celebration and we give thanks that our Goddess has given birth to the new sun. Our thoughts are with our own family at this time of the year so we wish each other a very peaceful and happy holiday.

And so we reach the worst part of the winter, keeping in touch with our friends and family, and making plans for the year ahead of us.

At the back of this book, I will give you a recipe for some very nice Yuletide Incense, which is very easy to make, some of the ingredients you may actually have in your store cupboard.

*Tuatha De Bridget is a Druidcraft Open Groven or Group in Glasgow. 'Druidcraft is in the valley where Druidry and Wicca meet.' (Philip Carr-Gomm)

The ceremonies in this book are a mix of Druidcraft, General Pagan, Shamanic and with touches of Heathen. Because of the normal mix of folks from different Pagan spiritual paths, I have tried to bring in as much as possible from different backgrounds. The Deity here is Celtic, from the Tuatha de Danann of Ireland. You can of course adapt this to your own chosen Deity or simply use a general term such as 'Lord and Lady'.

Part One — Wheel Of the Year

Imbolc

Imbolc Introduction

As Imbolc comes with the spring, with the first sign of snowdrops popping their heads through the ground, I am starting here.

Spring is the time of new beginnings. The ewes will come into milk ready to feed their lambs due to be born very soon. The days are longer now and the spring light is bright and sharp and the Sun is low in the sky.

This festival is associated with Brigit/Brigid; she is a Celtic Sun Goddess with a triple aspect. Unlike other Mother Goddesses, Brigit is said to have two sisters, the same age and governs Smith craft, Healing and Poetry. As a Fire Goddess, she is patron of Blacksmiths and is called upon to bless both the Blacksmith and his tools.

As a Healing Goddess, she is very much associated with birth, with the safe delivery of babies and indeed of animals. She is the Goddess who you would call to watch over you during labor and delivery. She is also involved with natural healing and herb craft and would be called upon to aid those employed making pills, lotions and potions.

Poetry is her gift and she would give this to her followers who asked in prayer and in meditation. Her followers, inspired by the Divine flow of her love and energy, have written many beautiful prayers and prose.

However, there is a dark side to all of this, as Goddess of the fire, the Hearth and the Blacksmith, just as fire burns and consumes, Brigit can lead her followers through the fire of destruction and on to the other side, like a Phoenix rising from the ashes. Fire purifies, it brings whole forests down to stumps of charcoal only for them to be fertilized into new growth. Brigit can take you all the way to the very bottom and then fill you with spiritual energy and re-growth, stronger and more able to continue.

In this first ceremony, we choose a girl or even a young woman who has not yet had any children. She plays the role of 'The Maiden'. She is crowned with a circlet of pure white flowers and asked during the ceremony to pour a libation of milk into the ground in honor of Brigit. For the sake of the general community, we do not normally dwell on the dark side of her, although I will share with you later a 'call', which I have written to be used in a Handfasting ceremony. For the moment let us celebrate the coming of the first milk, which will herald the arrival of the lambs on our farms.

Here is a checklist of what you will need to take with you to your ritual area and the different parts of the ceremony for several people to use. However, it would be just as easy to read all the parts yourself and do this as a solo ceremony. But let us go with the assumption that you have a group of friends, or a Grove or even a Coven.

Checklist for Imbolc Ceremony

Change of shoes, if you are going out into the park or countryside
Mobile phone to keep in touch with others travelling to the ceremony
Scripts, one for everyone present
Staff if required or Wand
Main Candle (White)
Candles to give out (white tea lights)
Candle lighter or matches
Incense
Charcoal
Cauldron or heatproof bowl
Tongs to hold charcoal

Small spoon for the incense

A Chalice

Bread or Cakes

Mead or Wine

Board or basket for the bread or cakes

Robes. (Perhaps better to wear warm clothes)

Cloak if you use one

First aid kit (a simple travel one should suffice but it is better to be prepared just in case)

Bowl for a libation to Brigit

Small container with milk for the libation.

Parts needed for the Imbolc Ceremony

Celebrant

Chant Leader/Circle

Earth

Sea

Sky

Ancestors

Spirit of Place

Brigit

*Maiden

Angus

*"Lucy" is the name given to a daughter of one of our group who wants to take an active part, even though she is only a girl. These little parts are ideal if you have a whole family coming along to your rituals and they all want to join in. Most of the time our "Lucy" does not have a speaking part, just little roles to play.

Imbolc Ceremony

Celebrant: There will be a short explanation of today's ritual and if necessary further parts will be allocated.

Circle: We will sing the circle into place by holding hands and pushing the energy right around the circle while we sing:

Let the circle be cast now and hold fast now, let the love of the Goddess be always in our hearts, merry meet and merry part and merry meet again. (x 3 times)

(We will ask our Druid to walk around the outside of the circle with her staff and shake the - bells as she goes).

Celebrant: Now the circle is cast and the fey have had bells rang to invite them into our circle we will begin.

Earth: I call to the solid, cold and frozen ground under my feet. You have held the seeds and bulbs for this spring all winter long, caring and watching them. Now you will release these and allow the earth to bring forth the wonder of nature. You are the foundation on which all of us stand, the stability, which enables us to walk. We acknowledge your strength and ask you to join with us now in this celebration of Imbolc.
Welcome to the realm of Earth!

All: Welcome Earth!

Sea: I call to the waters that surround us; the seas and the rivers that flow out into the sea.
You keep us in rhythm with the Moon, your tides ebbing and flowing, linking to us in emotion, sympathy and understanding. Throughout the year, you wash our shores a new, day by day. Now with the warmer days and the Sun's strength returning your waters will welcome back those that live in your waters, back to bring new life once more.
We understand your link to our emotions and we ask you now to strengthen this link in all of us so we may celebrate the season

and the wonder of new birth.

Welcome to the realm of Sea!

All: Welcome Sea!

Sky: I call to the Sky above our heads, the clear fresh air and the crisp breeze at springtime.

Within your realm are all the particles which allow us to breathe and without you we would not be able to survive. Your winds blow away the dark clouds of winter and bring us fresh new breeze. Your gales at this time of the year are said to come like a lion, strong and fierce, getting rid of many dead wood. But we know you will change to the gentleness of a lamb as the days move on.

Welcome to the realm of Sky!

All: Welcome Sky!

Ancestors: You are our ancestors. It is your gentle feet that have stood on this ground, who have walked this earth before us. You lived, worked and played here and we acknowledge your presence now.

Hail and Welcome!

All: Hail and Welcome!

Spirit of Place: (*shake rattle or beads*)

Welcome, Spirit of this place. It is your rivers that flow through this green place, into the sea.

Your energy that fills the harbors and allows the ships to sail. We feel your strength and your spirit.

Hail and Welcome!

All: Hail and Welcome!

Celebrant: Now that we have called to the three realms, to our ancestors and to the spirit of place, we will welcome Brigit and with her the first milk. We will sing a chant to welcome her now…

Chant

Brigit is waking; she's stirring and stretching,
Brigit is waking up from the snow.

Brigit come skip with, me your child I will always be,
Brigit come play with me, up from the snow. (x 3 times)
(to the tune of Mother Earth Carry Me)

(While we sing this chant members of the group will bring Brigit into the centre of the circle with her young maiden. Brigit and her young maiden will wind around the circle in and out of the group until they reach the place they started from.)

(Brigit reads a blessing and does a libation of milk, helped by her young maiden)

Brigit: As I slept, all has been quiet through the snows of winter. The light now returns and life begins anew. The first stirrings of the snowdrops from the mud and ice. The change in song of the birds whistling in the trees. The milk from the ewes as the lambs move, readying to be born.

I bless this milk, may this libation bring all of us closer and mindful of the ever-changing seasons.

(Maiden takes the milk from Brigit, pours the milk into the ground and hands the bowl back to Brigit.)

Maiden: The change in the season begins; there is work to be done.
May you keep the fire in your hearth well fed.
May you light the fire of your forge to burn with creativity.

May the light of the young sun gladden your hearts into song.

Rejoice! The year is returning with the growing light. Life will be abundant once more. Listen and you will hear my whisper of growing promise on the wind.

Angus: *(If possible the youngest male who can read aloud)* I am happy that you have chosen to wake and come play with us this day and I look forward to your strong growth and to the spring you will bring us.

(Brigit, her young maiden and Angus step back into the circle and join with the group for 'cakes and wine'.)

(Druid will bless and consecrate the mead and the bannock.)

The mead and bannock will be passed around the circle, the person who holds the chalice has the right to speak and make a toast if they wish, all others should allow them some quiet so they may speak and be heard.

Celebrant: A Poem for the Imbolc Ceremony

Brigit, Brigantia, the Most High.
The bringer of life after trials of deepest wintry slumber,
May your cauldron of plenty provide bounty for the year of promise ahead.

Brigit, Brigantia, the Most High.
The warrior and healer who does not rest until wholeness is assured,
Grant protection of mortals and beasts from the first birthings of spring.

Brigit, Brigantia, the Most High.

The enabler of green life giving earth and fresh waterways,
Heal our lands and renew the spirit life to our fertile pastures and fields.

Chant or Song: (*Time if possible for a second chant or song, everyone should join in and if they have rattles or drums, make a noise! Or play along if they wish.*)

Druid: (*Leads the chant*)
Spirits of the Earth,
Spirits taken form,
Rising to rebirth,
Rising to be born.

http://sites.google.com/site/potiaka/just-voice/SpiritsoftheEarth.mp3

Celebrant: It has now come to the time of our ceremony when we say goodbye or bid farewell to all those who have been called to this time and place.

Spirit of Place: (*shakes rattle*) Spirit of this place, it is your river that flows through this green place, into the sea. Your energy that fills the harbors and allows the ships to sail. From your rise in the hills to your meeting with Manannan in the Sea. We feel your strength and your spirit. We thank you for being with us today in this rite, now go if you must but stay if you will, we bid you Hail and Farewell!

All: Hail and Farewell!

Ancestors: You, who are our ancestors, and have walked this earth before us. It is your gentle feet that have stood on this ground. In the past you lived, worked and played and we thank you for your presence here today, go if you must but stay if you can, we bid you hail and farewell!

All: Hail and Farewell!

Farewell Sky:
I call with thanks to the Realm of Sky.

Thank you for filling our lungs with your fresh pure air, for allowing us all to enjoy this breath of early spring. Stay with us all as we go about our day to day lives and fill us with your intellect.

Farewell Sky!

All: Farewell Sky!

Farewell Sea:
I call with thanks to the Realm of Sea.

We are grateful for your ability to link with us in emotion and empathy. We love the way your rivers collect the rain and take it all the way out to the seas. Continue now to link us with the ebb and flow of the tides.

Farewell Sea!

All: Farewell Sea!

Farewell Earth:
I call with thanks to the Realm of Earth.

Your cold, solid foundation on which we all stand held us while we celebrated this early spring festival. Now allow the Sun to warm your ground, bring bright color to cheer us after this long winter. We will continue to do our best to look after you and we know you will always allow our fields and gardens to grow fresh flowers, vegetables and fruit.

Farewell Earth!

All: Farewell Earth!

Circle Closing Chant: (*We will ask our Druid to walk around the outside of the circle with her staff and bells and then come back into the circle to lead us singing the circle open.*)

May the circle be open, yet unbroken, may the love of the Goddess be always in our hearts, merry meet and merry part and merry meet again. *(sung x 3 times)*

GROUP HUG

Spring Equinox — Ostara

Spring Equinox Introduction

As the year turns, again we reach another time of balance, of equal day and equal night. At this time in the year, our group celebrates 'Ostara'.This meaning of this is explained in Wikipedia:

> Old English Ēostre (also Ēastre) and Old High German Ôstarâ are the names of a putative Germanic goddess whose Anglo-Saxon month, Ēostur-monath, has given its name to the festival of Easter ... Eostre is attested only by Bede, in his 8th century work De temporum ratione, where he states that Ēostur-monath was the equivalent to the month of April, and that feasts held in her honour during Ēostur-monath had died out by the time of his writing, replaced by the "Paschal month". The possibility of a Common Germanic goddess called Austrōn— was examined in detail in 19th century Germanic philology, by Jacob Grimm and others, without coming to a definite conclusion.
>
> Linguists have identified the goddess as a Germanic form of the reconstructed Proto-Indo-European goddess of the dawn, Hausos, some scholars have debated whether or not Eostra is an invention of Bede's, and theories connecting Eostre with records of Germanic Easter customs (including hares and eggs) have been proposed.

So we accept that the old Anglo-Saxon Goddess of the Spring was Ostara and that this name was eventually changed to 'Easter'. However it is at the Spring Equinox that we exchange colored eggs, hardboiled and painted or dyed, as well as the well known chocolate ones that are readily available in the shops at this time.

The timing of the Festival has also been changed to line up with the Jewish Passover and the Christian Easter, but we will not allow us to dwell over the ins and outs of why Easter is no longer at the Spring Equinox and why folks have forgotten the wonderful celebration of Ostara.

You will need a number of people to carry out this ceremony, or you may need to double up on the parts. We ask folk to bring along an egg, either one that they have dyed and painted or even a chocolate one. We put all of these into a central basket, which is blessed during the ceremony and then shared out to all who are present at the end. You could expand on this perhaps and suggest that some may want to bring either a wooden egg or a gemstone egg. It is possible to buy plastic eggs that you can fill with wild flower seeds. You can then ask people to go off and plant these seeds on spare ground or in cities where there are islands or little plots of land between roads. Some people mould the seeds with earth into a little ball and throw it out of the window along the sides of Motorways or Highways. You can see the result of this all over the British Isles as different councils have stopped cutting all the grass during the summer months and just cut a little edge to give people clear view of the side of the road.

This is a wonderful time of year for starting on a new course of study or for perhaps moving house, with such natural balance in the area, in the energy that flows naturally in very much lends itself to new starts.

It's also a very nice time for Baby Naming Ceremonies, especially when the new baby has siblings that can join in with the preparations by dyeing eggs or painting them or even perhaps making one from papier-mâché and decorating it.

If you are looking for such a ritual, I have included some towards the back of the book. But our ceremony here is to celebrate spring, balance, the new life we see around us in the wild, rabbits and birds.

Just a word about the Easter Bunny here; to our Pagan ancestors it was the hare who was the creature for this festival and it was thought that a hare would lay its eggs in a hollow on the ground. This originates from the fact that some land birds do look for an old lair made by a hare and use the soft fur that the mother hare pulls out of her coat to keep her babies warm. Therefore, it was a natural conclusion to these people that the eggs seen in these hollows in the ground did come from the hare.

The hare was the creature that it was thought witches would shape shift into, especially at the full moon at Ostara, thus it was considered for many years very bad luck to kill and eat a hare and it still is in some rural areas.

We all hope that an end is put to hare coursing, or in fact, to any so-called sport that involves hunting, chasing and killing a live creature for 'sport'. Nearly all Pagans love animals and all of nature, I have not met one single Pagan who would approve of killing an animal for fun. To feed your family, if they are hungry is a different thing. In some cultures if this is done, nothing is wasted and even the skin and the bones are put to good use to honor an animal that has been taken for food. All life if precious and it's important to remember that.

Just one more thing before we go on to the actual ceremony — eggs. Some people think that all eggs will grow into chicks if they are left with their mother, this is not the case. We only get fertilized eggs if the flock has a male bird running with the females. In the case of hens, no cockerel means no chicks; although the hens will still continue to lay eggs they are never going to become a baby chicks. If you are from farming stock you will know all this, but as many people now live in cities many have no idea at all that the eggs we buy from the supermarket, the brown free range kind are all acceptable. I once had this conversation with a man from an Indian background who would not eat any 'life', which included eggs. I explained all of this to him and he did agree that it was possible, if you knew for sure that the flock keeper had no cockerel, you would not be eating something that if left with the hen would hatch out as a chick. So let us assume now that all those you are going to use to hard boil, dye and paint, all come into this category.

Checklist for the Spring Equinox Ceremony
Decorated egg or small chocolate egg
Paper and pens
Cauldron
Incense
Charcoal
Tongs and spoon
Matches or lighter
Bowl to burn paper
Mead and oatcakes or bread
Chalice
Basket for the bread or cakes

Parts needed for the Spring Equinox Ceremony
Elder
East
South
West
North
Goddess
God
Spirit of Place
Ancestors

Spring Equinox Ceremony
We ask each person to bring an Egg (either decorated, wooden or chocolate). The Eggs will be exchanged at the end of the ceremony and will be blessed during the ritual.

While the circle is cast, one of the members of the group will read a circle casting prayer or if chosen the Elder, who is casting the circle, may wish to speak a few words as the circle is being cast.

Elder: Let us all be silent for a few seconds to gather our thoughts in order to celebrate this Spring Equinox Ceremony.

Call to the East: I call to the Spirit of the East, to the season of Spring, to the fresh clear air that blows around us with a gentle breeze. Welcome to the Lambs that have been born this Spring and to all young creatures, Welcome!

All: Welcome East!

Call to the South: I call to the Spirit of the South and to the season of Summer, we look forward later in the year to the long hot days of summer and to the mature animals, Welcome!

All: Welcome South!

Call to the West: I call to the Spirit of the West, to the vast open oceans and the mystical islands where our ancestors found peace and rest before their return. Bring to this Circle the qualities that you possess.
 We bid you, Hail and Welcome!

All: Hail and Welcome!

Call to the North: I call to the Spirit of the North, to the cold open spaces and the creatures that reside there. Bring to this Circle the qualities that you possess.
 We bid you, Hail and Welcome!

All: Hail and Welcome!

Leader: Let the Goddess, the God, the Spirits of this Place and our Ancestors be called also.

Call to the Goddess: I call to the Goddess of fertility who has awakened from her winter sleep. As her magic sweeps across the land bringing the surge of new life to all that reside upon her, we honor her and bring into harmony our lives with the coming of the new season. As the sap rises in all living things, the old is replaced by the new ... that is the way it was, and that is the way is will continue to be.

Welcome young Goddess into our Circle.

We bid you, Hail and Welcome!

All: Hail and Welcome!

Call to the God: I call to the God who through his seed the Goddess fulfils her magic at this time. Young man and lover share with us the power of your strength. Let us see and feel your presence in midst of these trees, and the energy and fecundity that you bring effect us all and we open our Circle to you.

Welcome young God into our midst.

We bid you, Hail and Welcome!

All: Hail and Welcome!

Call to the Spirit of Place: Beloved Clutha, gentle Spirit of this place, we gather here and honor your sacred land. As the 'green' begins to return to the land, and the leaves on the trees await the given time of opening, our hearts rejoice at the coming of the strengthening sun. Soon your wonderful valley will be vibrant with life again in honor of your name, and will once more be your 'dear green place'.

Welcome Clutha into our Circle.

We bid you, Hail and Welcome!

All: Hail and Welcome!

Call to the Ancestors: We give reverence to our Ancestors by inviting them to join with us today and share with us our joy and happiness at this Spring Equinox Ritual. Come join us and stand with us and allow us to feel your presence. We, your kin of line, blood and clan are honored to be here with you.

Cherished Ancestors join us if you will.

We bid you, Hail and Welcome!

All: Hail and Welcome!

Leader: Now that we are all assembled we can begin the body of our Spring Equinox Ritual ... starting in the North.

North: Now the day and night are in perfect balance. We stand at within the portal of dark and light.

East: Now we cast behind us the bleakness of winter and the past. We look forward to that which lies before us. Now is the time of planting seeds in the physical, mental and spiritual planes.

Leader: Take your piece of paper and write down goals for the coming year what you would like to achieve or have fulfilled. Think carefully about these for a few moments. Fold the paper up (not too tightly) and place it in the bowl.

(If it's possible the slips of paper will be burnt during the ritual, if not they will be burnt later and the ashes cast into a river

South: These are the seeds of our goals and desires. We place them in the hands of the Spirit of Place, Clutha, to present on our behalf before the Goddess and the God. May these desires and dreams be made manifest and become part of our lives.

West: May the very waters that bring life to this valley carry our thoughts and aspirations down to the Western Sea and beyond, that our deities and ancestors may take them and deal with them as they feel fit. We can be confident that our feelings are safe and will not return to us empty handed if our requests are honorable.

Leader: We are part of the renewal of life. Like all creatures, we are cherished and protected. May we grow in Love, Strength, Compassion and Wisdom, Children of the Goddess and the God. We are reborn as is Nature's way, and New Opportunities are lovingly presented before us.

(Bread and Mead will be passed around the Circle. Everyone should take a drink and a piece of bread in turn and make a toast as is the custom)

North: May the lands of Earth, her forests, rivers, seas and all creatures upon her be preserved and protected.

East: May the Earth be filled with Peace and Liberty

South: May the Earth be filled with Honor, Joy and Harmony.

West: May Love pervade all those who seek to serve. May our souls be forever united.

Leader: Let all those who were invited be thanked for their blessings and the circle opened.

Thanks to the Ancestors: I give thanks to the beloved Ancestors who gathered here with us today. Thank you for your presence and the qualities that you shared with us. Take with you our love and deepest respect as you return to the spirit world and remember us always, for we will not forget you. Stay if you will, but go if you must.

We bid you, Hail and Farewell!

All: Hail and Farewell!

Thanks to the Spirit of Place: Beloved Clutha, Goddess of our valley. We thank you for your presence and honor your land. May our thoughts and aspirations be welcomed as you carry them down to the God and the Goddess. Thank you Lady for being here with us this day.

We bid you, Hail and Farewell!

All: Hail and Farewell!

Thanks to the God: Lover and Consort, bringer of Joy and Fruitfulness. We thank you for being with us this day. May our lives always reflect the gifts you give us, and may we be ever mindful of your role in the turning of the seasons. We bid you, Hail and Farewell!

All: Hail and Farewell!

Thanks to the Goddess: I thank the Goddess for her presence, warmth and gentleness in bringing in each season at its given time. May we show that appreciation in our love of nature and its many faces over the turning wheel of the year. Praise be the young Goddess at this time of renewal.

We bid you, Hail and Farewell!

All: Hail and Farewell!

Thanks to the North: Blessings to the Spirit of the North for inspiring us with your presence. To the vast open spaces that leave us in awe and wonderment, and the many creatures that inhabit the wide open spaces.

We thank you for being here with us today.

We bid you, Hail and Farewell!

All: Hail and Farewell!

Thanks to the East: Blessings to the Spirit of the East for lifting our Spirits at this our Spring Equinox Ritual. To the rising of the life-giving sun and the joy that we all feel as each passing day lengthens. May our days be warm and our sky's be blue as we come out of winter into the budding season.

We thank you for being here with us today.

We bid you, Hail and Farewell!

All: Hail and Farewell!

Thanks to the South: Blessings to the Spirit of the South and the vision of long warm days and nights filled with the sounds and smells of nature. To the return of our feathered friends who winter in faraway place, and to the creatures that awake at the call of the rising temperatures.

We thank you for being here with us today.

We bid you, Hail and Farewell!

All: Hail and Farewell!

Thanks to the West: Blessings to the Spirit of the West the place of rest and renewal. To the seas and oceans that are vital for our very existence, and the varied creatures that reside therein that reminds us of how delicate our ecosystem really is. May your fluidity of thought stay with us reminding us of our part within nature and the responsibility we have as individuals.

We thank you for being here with us today.

We bid you, Hail and Farewell!

All: Hail and Farewell!

Leader: In the love of the God and the Goddess we gathered together to Celebrate this rite. May the God and the Goddess take the collective energy from this Circle and give it to the Trees under which we stand as a token of our love and appreciation for the privilege of being here. Blessed Be.

(The Circle will now be opened).

(Those who wish to share a song, a poem, a thought, now is the time).

GROUP HUG

Beltane

Beltane Introduction

This is the time of year when we celebrate the marriage of the Goddess to the God. It is the point in the year, which gives us the spark of fertility, of the creative flow. Traditions have long since been that a young woman, someone who has never had children or been married is chosen to represent the young Goddess. A young man is also chosen to be her partner.

Many of you will have read stories of young girls who have never been married who have been chosen to be the 'Bride' for Beltane. As for the May King, normally it is a young Stag, a young man who is himself unmarried but has reached the age that he could be chosen. Often someone in their twenties, fit and full of enthusiasm. In the stories we read, he is taken away, given a mask and has body paint applied all over his body, so much so that the young woman never really knows who he might be.

Then the maiden is also given a mask and a veil and is dressed and painted. The two people who are chosen will always have consented to this ceremony. The couple are then brought into the circle during the ceremony, bound together, as in a Handfasting and blessed. They then spend the next twenty-four hours together and their role is to enact the actual marriage of the God to the Goddess.

In these ancient times, at the end of this ceremony and feasting and dancing, the two young people would go back to their families or their tribes and not necessarily see each other again. Any children in early Pagan times always belonged to the Mother and if any babies were born from this ceremony, they were given a special magical name and taken great care of because the people felt these were the gifts of the Gods themselves.

These days we can't go about this in the same way, however our group does try and choose either a newly married couple or a couple who wish to be Handfasted for a year and a day. Although, as we have a high number of couples who have conceived after being chosen as May Queen and May King, we often have folk asking if they can take on these roles. We had one couple who had been told they were not able to have children, none of us knew this, and we chose them because they had just been married within the last month. Their first baby was conceived on the very night after our Beltane ceremony and they now have two beautiful children. So the magic is very powerful and if the Gods wish to bless a couple at this time of year, then it is very special.

The colors I always associate with Beltane is red, and orange-red, all the colors you would associate with fire, passion and strength. The flowers are nearly always red roses, or little red flowers, and the green is a bright vibrant emerald green. Ribbons of different shades of red are used and incense is specially blended with red rose petals in the mix.

We use Mead as a drink at Beltane especially because it is the chosen wine for a Handfasting — a Pagan Wedding. Enough Mead should be given to the Handfasted couple so that they can drink some each day for a full Lunar month, hence the term 'honeymoon'. But not all our chosen May Queens and May Kings do stay together, we do at times have to choose a young woman and a young man who are not a couple. In this last case, they merely play the part for the ceremony and then go their separate ways.

The ceremony I have written for this Beltane is a true Druidcraft ceremony. We are using the four directions and calling animals, birds or fish that we associate with these directions. It's possible that my chosen creatures are not the ones you would choose where you live, so I would suggest that you think about the animals or birds and fish which would mean a lot to you in the place you are living now. I live in Scotland and I've chosen these four because they very much connect with Scotland and Ireland, they are very Celtic.

You may feel that something more Wiccan would suit you or perhaps more Druid, and I will include some rituals at the back of the book that can be used at any time.

Check List for the Beltane Ceremony

Money for subs (needed for each gathering)
Change of shoes (if necessary)
Mobile phone to contact others travelling to the ceremony
Copy of the ceremony for everyone
Wand or staff
Main groups candle if used (if your group has its own candle it's a nice idea to take it along each time you have a ceremony)
Beltane Incense with cauldron
Tongs to hold charcoal and spoon
Charcoal
Mead and cakes or bread
Chalice
Basket for the bread or cakes
Wooden Athame
Small container to collect subs
First aid kit

Parts needed for the Beltane Ceremony

Elder 1
Elder 2
East/Osprey
South/Stag
West/Dolphin
North/Stallion
May Queen
May King (to be chosen by the May Queen)
Chant leader
High Priest and High Priestess to help with the Mead and Cakes if possible

Beltane Ceremony

We will first cast a circle, which will make a sacred space for the time of our ceremony. While this is being done the words of the Circle Casting Prayer will be read by .... (name)

Elder 1: We will now call to the directions and elements, also to the power animals of these elements.

Calls to the Elements

East: I call to the Air in the East, and ask for the power of the Osprey who lives in our hills and mountains to be with us, protect and guide us.

Welcome Sister Osprey!

All: Welcome Sister Osprey!

South: I call to the Fire in the South, and I ask for the strength of the Stag who guards his herd in our hills and valleys protect and guide us.

Welcome Brother Stag!

All: Welcome Brother Stag!

West: I call to the Water in the West, and I ask for the understanding of the Dolphin who swims in the seas around our coast, protect and guide us.

Welcome Sister Dolphin!

All: Welcome Sister Dolphin!

North: I call to the Earth in the North, and I ask for the stability of the Stallion that guards his herd in our valleys and fields. Protect and guide us.

Welcome Brother Stallion!

All: Welcome Brother Stallion!

HPS: Now let us call to Father Sun and Mother Earth.

Call to Father Sun

Father Sun, bright Lord of Beltane, be with us here today. As the grain fell to the reaper of harvest in Autumn, so now does the seed come forth from the darkness into light. Shine your light upon us, give us your potent power of life, bring us joy and love of life. Be with us today, be with us here, be with us now.

Welcome, Father Sun!

All: Welcome Father Sun!

Call to Mother Earth

Mother Earth, who gives life and shelter to us your children, who cradles us in your arms and washes us with your living waters. You who are old yet young, solid yet flowing, you who give us birth and receives us in death, let the light of your love shine upon us today, be with us here, embrace us in your fruitful glory, be with us now.

Welcome, O Mother Earth!

All: Welcome Mother Earth!

Elder 2: While we all calm down a little, we will tie some little ribbons onto our chosen May Queen for this year ... *(having first chosen a May Queen, those present will come forward and tie ribbons onto our May Queen)*

Elder 1: Its custom now for the May Queen to choose a mate, a Stag or a Friend who will help her for a year and a day, should she need any help. This help can be of all kinds, your mate this year may not be a conventional one, it may be someone who will help you in other ways, so May Queen, will you tell us who your May King or Mate is this year?

May Queen: Having thought about this for a while, I have chosen .... (name) to be my support, my help and my mate.

Elder 2: .... (name of chosen May King) Please step forward, (*waits for a moment or two while the May King joins the May Queen*).

Elder 1: .... (name) our May Queen has chosen you to be her support for a year and a day, you could be asked to go with her to places, to listen to her plans and her problems, to teach her and to work with her in magical ways, are you in agreement to all of this?

May King: .... (*name*)

Once we have the response from the chosen mate, we will briefly bind them with a cord in honor of this very old tradition.)

Chant: *Write or choose a chant, which can be repeated easily by your group.*

After this, Wine and Cakes will be blessed by the May Queen and King, with help from the HPS and HP and passed around the gathering.

HP: Now that we have shared the wine and cakes and celebrated this season of fertility and love, it is time to bid farewell to all those we have called to this time and space. To our ancestors of line, place and blood we thank you for joining us today, we bid you Goodbye!

All: Goodbye Ancestors!

Farewell to Mother Earth:
Mother Earth, bright mother of us all, your children bid you thanks. Goddess of the waters of life and bountiful mother of abundance, we thank you for your gifts. We thank you for your presence here today; go if you must but stay if you will; Goodbye Mother Earth!

All: Goodbye Mother Earth!

Farewell to Father Sun:
Father Sun, lord of the fire, we have kindled the flame of your bel-fire and your love here today. Let your light shine upon and within us so that we may reach the harvest of our lives. We thank you for your presence here today; go if you must but stay if you will, Goodbye Father Sun!

All: Goodbye Father Sun!

North: Brother Stallion, thank you for your stability with your presence here this evening, go if you must, but stay if you will, Goodbye Brother Stallion!

All: Go if you must but stay if you will, Goodbye Brother Stallion!

West: Sister Dolphin, thank you for your understanding and your presence here this evening, go if you must, but stay if you will, Goodbye Sister Dolphin!

All: Go if you must but stay if you will, Goodbye Sister Dolphin!

South: Brother Stag, thank you for your strength and protection here this evening, go if you must but stay if you will, Goodbye

Brother Stag!

All: Goodbye Brother Stag!

East: Sister Osprey, thank you for your protection and your presence here this evening, go if you must but stay if you will, Goodbye Sister Osprey!

All: Go if you must, but stay if you will, Goodbye Sister Osprey!

The circle will be opened as the words of the Circle Opening Prayer are read.
Please remain in the circle until these words are sung:

All: The Circle is open, yet unbroken, may the love of the Goddess be always in our hearts, merry meet and merry part, and merry meet again. (sung x 3)

GROUP HUG

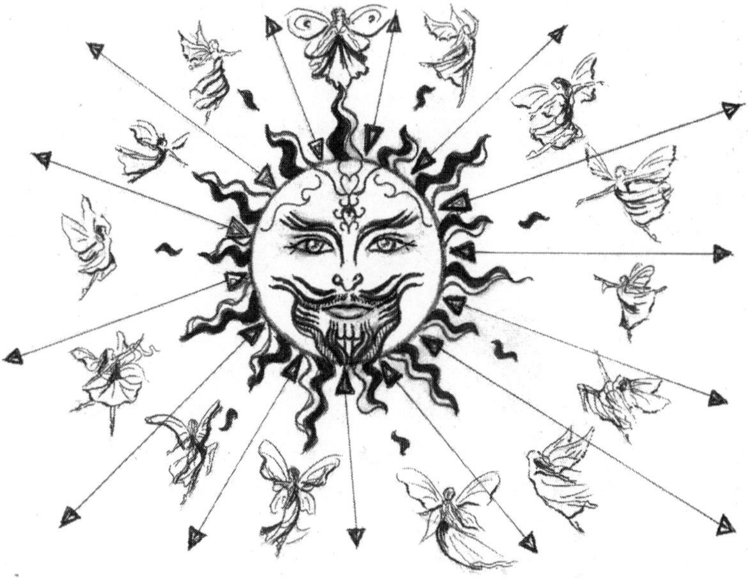

Summer Solstice

Summer Solstice Introduction

This is the high point of the summer, the very longest day and shortest night and we meet to celebrate this very special day. The Sun is at its strongest point and the God at his greatest strength.

You will no doubt find other pieces of acting to do within a wheel of the year festival. Other books will talk of fights between the Oak King and the Holly King, but I am leaving these out for a good reason, I want the reader and user of this book to connect deeply and directly to the realms and to the elements, animals, birds and fish associated with them. Once you have a much deeper connection, you may then wish to go on to include other traditions from your area of the World.

As with all the main points of the wheel of the year it has always been a time when our ancestors met together, celebrated and were often visited by their Priests, Druids and Elders. If any special celebration were to be added, then it would be done in the middle of the ceremony, a Baby Naming perhaps or even a Handfasting. Perhaps a young man might have reached his manhood and it was time for him to leave childhood pastimes behind and this would be acknowledged. A big fuss would be made of the young man who would perhaps then be required to work in the fields or hunt with his father and brothers.

It's perhaps one of the best times of the year for such a rite of passage for a young man and he perhaps would choose to take a magical name and be accepted as an adult member of the tribe. You will find rites of passage towards the end of the book and all you need do is slot them into the ceremony just before the 'cakes and wine' section.

The words at the start, spoken by the Elder for this festival teaches us a great deal more about this time of year, this piece was written by a Druid member of our group and I have left this piece as it was written and read.

Check list for the Summer Solstice Ceremony

Money for subs
Change of shoes (if necessary)
Mobile phone to contact members travelling to the ceremony
Copy of script for everyone
Wand or staff
Summer Solstice Incense with cauldron
Tongs to hold charcoal and spoon
Charcoal
Lighter of matches
Main candle
Chalice
Mead or Wine
Bread
Basket of board for the bread
Small container to collect subs
First aid kit

Parts needed for the Summer Solstice Ceremony

Elder
Maiden/Lucy: *'Lucy' is the name given to our group's young maiden, the daughter of one of our members, you may perhaps have someone with a young daughter or grand daughter who is very keen to take part and these little roles are ideal.*
Spirit of place
Earth
Sea
Sky
Chant leader/Potia: *Potia is one of the original founder members of our group and has a web page with chants you can download and use for these ceremonies if you wish. Or you may have someone with their own chants you can use in these places?*

Ancestors
Brigantia
Belenus
Speaker 1
Speaker 2
Speaker 3
Speaker 4

There are more parts in this ritual than some of the other festivals so it may be necessary to ask people to read more than one part.

Summer Solstice Ceremony

Elder: We gather to celebrate the time of the longest day when the sun is at its peak. The Summer Solstice is the time when the sun appears to pause on its eternal journey, held between the waxing and waning year. At this time, our ancestors gathered in celebration. They lit bonfires at sunset in honor of the sun, whose power is at its greatest at this time. They danced, sang, shared food and drink and when the embers were low they jumped over them to ensure a good harvest and protection from summer storms. They also rolled fiery wheels made of straw down the hillsides to re-enact the passage of the sun across the sky as it starts it journey towards the southern horizon. It was considered good luck if these wheels were extinguished in the waters of a river.

This time of year was also a time for gathering herbs associated with the sun. St John's Wort, Vervain, Mugwort, Yarrow and Ferns were collected at this time for their medicinal and magical powers. People made midsummer wreaths, which they gave as gifts or hung around the neck of their cattle as a protection against misfortune.

Couples also pledged their love to each other at this time of year. In some places, vows were spoken with hands joined through a hole in special stones. And the fairy folk were also said to be out in the warm evenings, dancing and singing. So as we stand under the eye of the sun, let us gather in celebration as our ancestors did.

As gift to the fairy folk and the spirits of this place, I am going to ask Lucy to move round the circle and blow bubbles for us all. As she does this, I'd like each of you to think about the fragile beauty of bubbles, the wonderful mix of air and water shimmering in the light, dancing over the earth. Look for the colors dancing on their skin. Rejoice in the beauty and live in that moment. Let the simple joy of being alive under the summer sun rise up with you. Let it burst out of you and share it with those around you.

Elder: Let us cast a circle to bless this area and to create a barrier between this World and the World of the Ancient ones.

(The Elder will walk around the outside of the circle, casting and asking for a blessing of safety for those who are about to perform this ceremony and after her one of the young people)

Lucy *(our young maiden) walks round the circle blowing bubbles for us all.*

Call to Spirit of Place: Spirit of this place, energy that flows in and around us, honor and respect is yours from us and we welcome you into our circle. Welcome!

All: Welcome!

Elder: Let us call with respect to the spirits of Earth, Sea and Sky and strengthen our connections to them.

Earth, Sea and Sky step forward into the centre to do their calls

Earth: We give honor to the firm Earth beneath our feet. We have great respect for the way in which you hold us safe. Spirits of the Earth we welcome you into our circle today, Welcome!

All: Welcome!

Sea: Let us give honor to the Spirits of the Seas, the Waters of Life flowing through us and through the Land. Let its fluidity so full of emotion help us to connect with each other. Spirits of the Sea, we welcome you into our circle today, Welcome!

All: Welcome!

Sky: Let us give honor to the Spirits of the Skies, the sparkling heavens above us. Let us increase our awareness to the Universe. Help us to know the wonders and openness that are part of the Skies and of us. Welcome to the spirits of the Skies! Welcome!

All: Welcome!

Earth, Sky and Sea step back into circle.

All join in with chant Earth Sky and Sea *written by Potia:*

Earth, Sky and Sea
These are the three
Earth, Sky and Sea
All within me.
(repeated)

Earth is my flesh
All things do mesh

Sea is my blood
Tears also flood

Sky is my soul
All things made whole

Earth, Sky and Sea

These are the three
Earth, Sky and Sea
All within me.
(repeated)

Elder: Let us now call upon the ancestral Spirits of this place, of our families and of the Spiritual paths we follow.

Ancestor call: Ancestors of this sacred place, ancestors of our blood and spirit, all those of the Land of Brighid and all ancestors of this earth we stand upon, all those who watch over this circle and stand with their hands to our backs, we ask you to join our circle on this summer solstice and bid you Hail and Welcome!

All: Hail and Welcome!

Elder: Let us call upon our Brigantia and Belenus and ask for their Presence in this rite.

Call to Brigantia:
Beloved Brigantia, you who are Mistress of hearth and home, protector of family and tribe, we ask you to join with us this day as we celebrate the summer solstice. Hail and Welcome!

All: Hail and Welcome!.

Call to Belenus:
The sun is high above us
shining down upon the land and sea,
making things grow and bloom.
Great and powerful Belenus—
we honor you this day—
and thank you for your gifts.
You are known by many names.

You are the light over the crops in the fields,
the heat that warms the earth,
the hope that springs eternal,
the bringer of life.
We welcome you, and we honor you this day,
celebrating your light,
as the wheel turns and we begin our journey once more
into the darkness.

All: Hail and Welcome!

Elder: Let us reflect for a while on the sun.

Speaker 1: The sun is the Child of Heaven, the son of the bright day, the day star that shines in the darkness of space. He is the light that chases away the shadows and shows us what truly is. He is the eye, the Bright One, the many-skilled, the teacher. Happy are we who learn from his hand.

Speaker 2: The sun is the Lover of the Earth. She is the rosy dawn, the exalted one who's light and warmth brings fruitfulness to the land. She is the gentle embrace that enfolds the world. She gives of herself freely,; her golden rays bring the promise of the harvest to come. We are blessed by the gift of her love.

Speaker 3: The sun is the Heart of Love. He is the lover that ignites the fires of passion, the golden shower that descends from heaven. He frees us of our fears and wraps us in the cloak of his protection. In his arms, we are truly alive with the joy of life. In his eyes, we are remade in truth and beauty.

Speaker 4: The sun is the Mind of Light. She is knowledge and understanding, the beauty of words and the strength of bronze. She fires the forge of reason and intellect but tempers her gift in the waters of inspiration. We glow golden in the light of her fires. We shine in the radiance of her creation.

Elder: The sun is the Power of Life. He is the seed, the hidden promise waiting for her light to fall upon him. She is the creatrix, the power that moves the world. We breathe her breath, her gift of life. His blood flows within us; his spirit shines within our hearts. We share in the cycles of their lives.

Elder: As part of this rite, we will share bread and mead together, fruits of the earth warmed by the sun.

Mead and bread will be blessed by two of those present in the circle and circulated round the circle. When you receive the cup you can make a toast and either drink or offer a libation if you choose. If you do not wish to do either, simply pass the cup to the next person along. The bread follows the cup and you can either take a bit to eat or break it into crumbs to scatter. Again, if you don't wish to do either just pass it along. The cup and bread will keep circulating until all the mead has gone. The traditional toast from the person who gets the last drink is 'To the Last Drops'. When this toast is made, the cup and whatever remains of the bread should be brought back into the centre.

Elder: Now we have shared in the fruits of the earth, let us share in a song.

   (*a suitable song which has been chosen is now sung and shared by all*)

Elder: Let the gods be thanked for their presence with us today.

Thanks to Belenos:
As we leave this Circle in harmony, we bid farewell to the Sun God Belenus. The light filters this place with green hews.
   The smell of the woods adds magic in the air.
   Birdsong and the constant sound of buzzing insects fills our

senses and delights us.

The world would be bland and dead if the magic of the God and Goddess didn't permeate through the seasons at their appointed time.

Belenus, we bid you Hail and Farewell!

Thanks to Brigantia: We thank you for being here with us today, for surrounding us in your love. We ask that you stay with us as we go back into our mundane world. We bid you Hail and Farewell!

All: Hail and Farewell!

Elder: Let our ancestors be thanked for their presence among us.

Thanks to Ancestors: We give thanks to the Ancestors today for joining us and protecting us. We feel their presence in this circle and thank them for their loving and healing energy. May we take their love, warmth and embraces with us that we have felt today. So may it be!

All: So may it be!

Elder: Let us give thanks to the Spirits of Earth, Sky and Sea and for our connections with them.

Earth, Sky and Sea move into the center again.

Sky: We give thanks to the spirits of Sky for helping us feel the wonder and openness of the Universe. May we carry with us the quickness of thought and knowledge we have gained today. Farewell Sky!

All: Farewell!

Sea: We give thanks to the spirits of the Seas for helping us feel the flexibility and fluidity and emotion within our lives. May we continue to show our empathy with others as you have shown us today. Farewell Sea!

All: Farewell!

Earth: We give thanks to the spirit of the Earth for helping us feel your strength and solidity as part of us. May we always feel your stability beneath our feet. Farewell Earth!

All: Farewell!

Earth, Sky and Sea move back into the circle.

Elder: Let us give thanks to the Guardian Spirit of this place.

Thanks to Spirit of Place:
We thank you ancient Spirit of this Place for welcoming us into your presence once more and for joining with us for this special day. For now we bid you Hail and Farewell!

All: Hail and Farewell!

Elder will open the circle.
(the Elder walks around the outside of the circle thanking the circle for its protection during the rite and asks that it dissolve and leave no trace behind.)

Lughnasadh or Lammas

Lughnasadh Introduction

For those of us living in Europe, this time of year is the corn Harvest and there are many different traditions associated with it. It's a time to give thanks to the Deity, to Nature and perhaps to rejoice in the fact we have a harvest to gather in. We see in this ceremony that the corn king is cut down, and departs into the earth and in our eyes to the Summerlands. So it's the first of the Harvest Festivals and as such you might wish to bake a fancy loaf of bread. A braid made with raised dough and then baked in a hot oven looks very good in the middle of the circle or perhaps you may be lucky enough to have someone who can make a sheaf of corn in bread.

If your first harvest is different from this, if you live in a different part of the World, then you will no doubt have to adapt this ceremony. It would be very simple to swap the corn for whatever it is in your part of the World and to add a 'King' of your chosen food. The whole idea of all these ceremonies is that it leads us all through the year, connects us to the spirits of the place we live and work in and to the natural cycle of the year.

Your local traditions may be different from ours, or may even be stronger. Perhaps you make corn dollies or Sun wheels in your area. If you do have this kind of tradition, it is perhaps a good idea to hold a meeting during the week in the run up to the ceremony and sit around and make Sun Wheels and Corn Dollies. Alternatively, have a weekend camp and on the Saturday get someone to come along to teach how to do these things and then hold your celebration on the Sunday.

You will need the usual collection of items for any ceremony, plus the special bread, a Sun incense, and once again, if you are also holding a rite of passage within this celebration, then you need to bring all you want for this as well.

Check List of items needed for the Lughnasadh Ceremony

Directions to the site

Compass to find the directions, or application on your smart phone

Wand or Staff

Sun or Lughnasadh Incense

Cauldron

Charcoal, tongs and a spoon

Matches or lighter

Main candle

Bread and Mead or Wine

Basket or board to hold bread

Copies of ceremony for each person

Parts needed for the Lughnasadh Ceremony

Leader

East

South

West

North

Spirit of Place

Ancestors

Goddess

God

Speaker 1

Speaker 2

Speaker 3

Speaker 4

Lughnasadh Ceremony

It is always a very good idea to start each festival with a word of explanation for all those gathered together. You and your friends will be very familiar with all of this but if you are holding an open ritual or you have

invited guests, it's by far the best thing to have your leader talk to everyone present to start with and explain what is about to happen and ask them to come over and stand in a circle.

Circle casting: *(the chosen Leader will walk around the outside of the circle, blessing and casting as he or she goes. Or you may find it better to ask a Priestess to do this while the Leader reads the short prayer?)*

Leader: We cast this circle here today,
to celebrate our Lughnasadh rite.
Let Love, Light and Harmony prevail,
As we do will, so mote it be!

East: Ancient spirit of the East,
Whose element is air,
The mighty hawk soaring in the skies,
Be with us now to watch over our rite,
Hail and Welcome!

All: Hail and Welcome!

South: Ancient spirit of the South,
Whose element is fire,
The majestic stag in the heat of the chase,
Be with us now and watch over our rite,
Hail and Welcome!

All: Hail and Welcome!

West: Ancient spirit of the West,
Whose element is water,
The magnificent salmon who swims upstream,
Be with us now and watch over our rite,
Hail and Welcome!

All: Hail and Welcome!

North: Ancient spirit of the North,
Whose element is Earth,
The mysterious boar who lives in the forest,
Be with us now to watch over our rites.
Hail and Welcome!

All: Hail and Welcome!

Spirit of Place: May the Goddess of our beautiful river and valley bless our gathering this day. Clutha of this green place be with us now as we celebrate this time of first harvest, Lughnasadh. Be with us and touch us with your presence. Weave within our circle bringing power and purpose to our ritual, blessing the earth beneath our feet as we tread this path together. Hail Clutha and Welcome!

All: Hail and Welcome!

Ancestors: We call and invite our ancestors of line, blood and place to stand with us in circle. May our lives be made rich by your presence and our connection to the land strengthened, and the ancient tales and stories that bind us as one deepen our love for our past and a hope for all our futures. We bid you Hail and Welcome!

All: Ancestors Hail and Welcome!

Goddess: We stand in circle today to honor our Great Mother who loves and cares continually for her children. Therefore, we ask for her blessing on our rite and to accept our love for the abundance that she gives freely. We bid you Hail and Welcome!

All: Hail and Welcome!

God: Blessings on you, Father of the Land. We honor your presence today and the great sacrifice that you are to make to ensure that life continues into the next year. May our love go with you as you bleed into the land and may your journey into the underworld be smooth and without sorrow. With much sadness, we bid you Hail and Welcome if only for a short time.

All: Hail and Welcome!

Speaker: The name Lughnasadh is Irish Gaelic and means the assembly of Lugh. Lughnasadh was one of the cross quarter festivals of the Celtic year, along with Samhain, Imbolc, and Beltane. The festival seems to have included tribal assemblies and activities. According to historical evidence, it was only celebrated in Britain, Ireland, France (ancient Gaul), and possibly Northern Spain.

Speaker 2: Today, Pagans celebrate Lughnasadh as one of the eight festivals in the witches' Wheel of the Year, but many know little about it beyond the fact that it marks the beginning of harvest. Unlike May Day, Yule or Midsummer relatively few of its customs survive either in folklore or historical record. Nevertheless, even in these times of all-year-round imported fruit and crops, its presence can still be felt. If we dig deep enough, we can still find its traces.

Speaker 3: So is Lughnasadh relevant today, and should we as Pagan's celebrate it? Well, its influence is still felt on our modern patterns of both work and leisure. Within living memory Factory and school holidays were timed to coincide with the start of the harvest so that more people would be free to help with the harvesting. Even in today's post-industrial age, early August, in Great Britain remains the traditional time for summer holidays and fairs. Another and more important reason is this. Our religious practices are born of myth and legend that stem from the very land itself. Our forefathers saw the wisdom and magic in the turning of the Year and celebrated each time, at its appointed time, the moment when Lugh touched the Earth and ripened the harvest for that season.

Speaker 4: During the not so distant past, it was deemed necessary to alter the calendar and so in today's calendar, the festival of Lughnasadh falls around the 1st of August. Before the calendar was changed it was about the 14th. So, in keeping with tradition and convenience, we are celebrating our Lughnasadh celebration on the nearest Sunday to the older date.

Leader: It is time to honor the Earth Goddess of the bountiful harvest,
The Mother of all that lives and breathes,
Providing you with the fruits and grains for your sustenance.
The Cereal is ripe in our fields,
Its golden countenance dancing in the sun.
It is your time for harvest,
Your time to break the bread and share the feast,
Time to honor the Sun God Lugh as he sacrifices himself for our continuing life.

(John Barleycorn, can be sung or played if a member of the gathering has the talent to do this for us.)

Bless the bread and wine: *(It's normal in our group for the people who are taking the part of the Goddess and the God to also bless the bread and wine, but you can choose to offer this role to elders or perhaps to visitors if you wish)*

I bless this bread/wine in the presence of the Great Mother the Gracious Goddess and Lugh the Radiant God, so mote it be!

The bread and then the wine is now passed around to all in the circle *(deosil which is sunwise)*.

God: With tears in our eyes and appreciation in our hearts for the sacrifice you have made for all creation for we now know that you must depart into the underworld, we bid you Hail and Farewell!

All: Hail and Farewell!

Goddess: Great Mother of abundance, we are mindful of your love for us and thank you for blessing our circle with your presence. Go if you must, but stay if you will, we bid you Hail and Farewell!

All: Hail and Farewell!

Ancestors: May we bid farewell to our beloved ancestors until we meet again. Go if you must, but stay if you will, we bid you Hail and Farewell!

All: Hail and Farewell!

Spirit of Place: Gracious Clutha we thank you for your presence this day. Go if you must, but stay if you will, we bid you Hail and Farewell!

All: Hail and Farewell!

(The four quarters are thanked and dismissed)

North: Ancient spirit of the North,
Whose element is Earth,
The mysterious boar who lives in the forest,
Thank you for your presence,
Hail and Farewell!

All: Hail and Farewell!

East: Ancient spirit of the East,
Whose element is air,
The mighty hawk soaring in the skies,
Thank you for your presence,
Hail and Farewell!

All: Hail and Farewell!

South: Ancient spirit of the south,
Whose element is fire,
The majestic stag in the heat of the chase,
Thank you for your presence,
Hail and Farewell!

All: Hail and Farewell!

West: Ancient spirit of the west,
Whose element is water,
The magnificent salmon who swims upstream,
Thank you for your presence,
Hail and Farewell!

All: Hail and Farewell.

(Anyone now who has brought a poem or a piece of prose, song or chant to share with us all, please now share them and let us all enjoy.)

Leader: We close this magical circle that we earlier created.
Let this barrier between this World and the next disappear and leave no trace, from above to below.
So mote it be!

All: So mote it be!

Leader: This celebration is ended in peace as it began; merry meet, merry part, and merry meet again.

GROUP HUG

It is a nice idea to get everyone to link with each other and take a step forward into the circle to have a group hug!

Most of this ceremony has been written by my partner, Piet Ceanadach. As he made such a good job of it, I have chosen to add this into the collection.

Autumn Equinox

Autumn Equinox Introduction

At the last festival, we celebrated the first of the harvests, the corn grain at Lughnasadh, and now we have reached the second harvest which is the apple and pear, with the first of the berries also coming ripe. It's a very special time and was so for our ancestors because they would store their apples all through the winter and eventually they might only have had apples and cheese left to eat until the spring. The apple is a very magical fruit as is shown if you cut the fruit in half width ways, open it up and look at the middle where you will see a five pointed star or pentagram made by the pips.

Apples really are very nourishing, and with the addition of a piece of cheese make a light meal, especially for anyone travelling.

A word about the bee's role in all of this, it's not the just honey they produce to make mead and to eat which is important, bees are very important to all our lives because it's the humble bee that pollinates the apple blossom, which in turn gives us our apples in the Autumn. We always drink a toast to the bees, and I hope you will do also? With a nasty virus at the moment killing off hundreds of hives all over the world, we can only hope that soon a cure can be found to help them or in the future we will have very few fruit or vegetables to make a harvest, or even in fact to live on.

This time your checklist to take with you is a little different because you need no bread or cakes, apples take their place. You will also need a basket to put all your apples in and although I would advise you not to take blades into the woods, it seems to upset the elementals, on this occasion you are going to need a knife to cut an apple in half for all to see.

The ceremony is different this time as we are calling to the spirits of the animals and when we call Deity we are simply using the terms: Father Sky and Mother Earth. On this occasion you need not make a circle, you can stand in whatever shape you feel is comfortable, neither do you need to be in any special direction to call to the spirit animals, although if you are in a group of people it's always nice to have folks standing in different areas rather than all together.

One last point, you will see the need for a shaker here, and if you don't have one, the easiest way to make one I have found is to fill an empty plastic jar, the kind you might get vitamins in, fill it with lentils, put the lid on tight and put the filled jar into a little cloth bag. It makes a very nice shaker.

The sound of the sea is a little more difficult and requires a long flat container and sand with grit, once all sealed inside if you tip the container slowly from one side to another, you should get a sound like the waves rolling onto the shore. You can buy an ocean drum but it's great fun having a go at making them.

Check List for the Autumn Equinox Ceremony

Map to venue of site
Compass or application on your smart phone
Autumn Incense, cauldron, charcoal, tongs and spoon
Matches or lighter
Main group candle
Staff or Wand
Cider
Shamanic rattle
Sea sound maker
Apples
Mead or Wine
Poem or song to share

Parts needed for the Autumn Equinox Ceremony

Elder
Spirit of place
Fox

Seal
Eagle
Ancestor
Father Sky
Mother Earth
Spirit of the Apple Tree

Autumn Equinox Ceremony

It's always a good idea to have a word with everyone present and let them know what is about to happen and what style this ceremony will take.

Elder: *(walks into the center of the area being used and bangs a staff on the ground, three times)* I declare this area special and sacred for the duration of our ceremony.

Spirit of Place: I speak to the guardian spirit of this place, the Whyte and ask that you accept this gift of cider.
(Pours a cup of Cider onto the ground as a libation to the spirit).
You are the spiritual body who cares so deeply for this area and we wish you no harm. Come amongst us now and join with us as we celebrate this season.

All: Welcome Spirit of Place!

Fox: *(Shakes a rattle or uses some other item to make a noise and attract the Fox Spirit)* Sister Fox, you guard your cubs so carefully, we ask you to join us now and help guard us while we celebrate this season. Welcome Sister Fox!

All: Welcome Sister Fox!

Seal: *(Makes a noise like the waves of the sea)* Sister Seal, so many stories have been written about you, how you provide for your children, even your human children. I ask you now to provide a safe space for us today, bring us the nourishment we need to learn more. Welcome Sister Seal!

All: Welcome Sister Seal!

Eagle: *(Make a noise like the wind)* Brother Eagle, you soar high above us on air currents, you see even the smallest movement and your hunting skills are legend. Watch out for us from high above the ground, help us to see with your eyes, join with us as we celebrate this festival. Welcome Brother Eagle!

All: Welcome Brother Eagle!

Call to the Ancestors: We call to our ancestors, those of our family and friends who have gone on to the Summerlands. We call to those of our bloodline, to which we belong by marriage and by choice. And lastly, I call to the ancestors who lived and worked in this special place, those whose feet stood on the same ground we stand on today and I ask you to be with us now and watch over this ceremony. I bid you Hail and Welcome!

Elder: Let us speak to our spirit parents, to Mother Earth and Father Sky and ask them to join us.

Father Sky: You are the power behind the turning of the year Father Sky; it is you who sends the Sunlight that warms the Earth. Although we know you are all around us, we turn our heads upwards when we think of you. Your power fires the Stag when time comes for the rut, hormones flow and passions rise. Come amongst us now Father Sky and fill us with your passion, fire us with enthusiasm so that we may celebrate as the year turns from Summer into Autumn. Welcome Father Sky!

All: Welcome Father Sky!

Mother Earth: Mother Earth, your mantle is changing from fresh green into the many shades of Autumn or Fall. Green turns to copper and yellow, copper turns to brown, the mornings are heavy with dew and your spiders come out to spin great webs. But still the Sun shines brightly during the day, and the nights become colder with frost in the morning. Mother your fruits have nourished us all year and now you give us a great harvest of apples. Your loving care surrounds us and we ask you to stay with us now as we celebrate this season, welcome Mother Earth!

All: Welcome Mother Earth!

Elder: The time of the Autumn Equinox is also a time of harvest when apples are gathered from the orchards and brambles, rose hips and sloes are collected from the hedgerows. Now that we have spoken to the spirit animals and to our spiritual parents, let us learn more about this season.

Let us rejoice in the turning of the wheel and the changing seasons. Let us celebrate this time of harvest. Let us welcome the Spirit of the Apple Tree into our circle.

Spirit of the Apple Tree: I am the spirit of the Apple Tree, I have stood on this earth for many years and my own ancestors stood here before me. When I came into blossom in the spring, many bees visited me and brought me different pollen and in exchange, I gave some of my own pollen. This has fertilized me and now I am bending with the weight of so many apples. These are my gift to you; they will help nourish you all though the winter months and I have a secret to share with you.

Take one of my apples and cut it in half across the middle from side to side, in the centre you will see its pips, the seeds for new trees. But here lies a secret, you will see five seeds making a star inside the apple. This star is for all the elements on the Earth and for the Spirit of Creativity that binds everyone and everything together. Learn this secret, go away and spend your winter reading about all of this and grow in understanding and you will learn to live in harmony with all of creation. Harmony must be your goal this season and spread this out as you go.

I am the spirit of the Apple Tree and I send you my blessings!

All: Thank you Apple Tree for your words and for your apples!

(You should have a bowl of apples on the ground in the area you are working and the Elder or other chosen person should bless these apples and give the bowl to one of the younger folks to pass around for all to share. 'Lucy' who is our young maiden will do this task for our group.

It's a very nice idea if you have children who come along with their parents or guardians and want to play a part in the ceremony to let them do these tasks. If they are keen then to carry fruit, or at times to carry a candle and bring people a 'light' is a very nice role for young folk to take.)

Chant
Spirit of the Apple Tree, let your spirit flow here free (rep at least three times).

Blessing of Bread and Mead, this can be done in a simple manner or can be done in a more ritual Wiccan way. If you are doing this for the first time then a simple:

I bless this Mead and these cakes/bread in the names of my Goddess and God *(insert patron names)* and I ask that these will nourish us both in a physical manner and in a spiritual way as we all join in this together.

Blessed Be!

Anyone close who hears these words should react with 'Blessed Be' in response.

Elder: If any of you have written a poem or have a song you want to sing to us, now is the time. Has anyone anything to share today?

(Go around the circle in a Sunwise direction and give folks the chance to read their poems, sing their song or simply share something about this time of year.)

Elder: Let us thank and bid farewell to all those we have called into our grove today.

Thanks to the Spirit of the Apple Tree:
I wish to thank the spirit of the Apply Tree for sharing your wisdom with us today and helping us understand the magical wonders of your fruit. I bid you Farewell!

All: Farewell!

Thanks to the Spirit of Place:
I thank the guardian of this place for staying with us, protecting us and adding your energy to ours, until we meet again. Farewell Spirit of Place!

All: Farewell!

Thanks to the Ancestors:
I speak with thanks to our ancestors of line, blood and place. We are all glad that you came to join us and we know that you are only a thought away beyond the veil. Farewell Ancestors!

All: Farewell!

Thanks to our Spiritual Parents

Father Sky: We feel your power, your warmth and strength, and we know you have been with us today, as you are always when we call. Continue to give your strength to the Stag in the heat of the rut and give us this strength of passion also. Farewell Father Sky!

All: Farewell Father Sky!

Mother Earth: We will watch as your cloak changes from its rich green to the mellow hues of bronze, gold and brown. The apples and your harvest have nourished us and for this we thank you. Now go if you must but stay if you can. Farewell Mother Earth!

All: Farewell Mother Earth!

Eagle: Brother Eagle *(make a noise like the wind)*, soaring high above us on the wind, you have seen the slightest movement and have been able to protect us and we want to thank you. You are welcome to stay amongst us if you wish Brother Eagle, but for this ceremony we wish you Farewell!

All: Farewell Brother Eagle!

Seal: Sister Seal *(make a sound like the sea)*, we are all aware of how well you provide for us and watch out for us. It's time now for us to say good bye from this ceremony, although please know that you are always welcome in our circle. Farewell Sister Seal!

All: Farewell Sister Seal!

Fox: Sister Fox *(shake the rattle to attract the Fox Spirit)*, you have stood guard over us and we know how well you provide for your children, thank you for all you do for us in this World and from the Spirit World. Farewell Sister Fox!

All: Farewell Sister Fox!

Spirit of Place: Spirit of this place, we wish to thank you for allowing us to use your area and for staying with us and helping to guard us. Farewell Spirit of Place!

All: Farewell!

Elder: *(Walks into the centre of the area that has been used today and bangs his staff on the ground.)*
I declare this sacred space, made holy for our ceremony be now returned to this time and place. Let no trace be found here that this has been used for ceremony.

GROUP HUG

Before everyone leaves, it's a very good idea to just check all the things that have been used have been picked up from the ground. Leave some apple for the birds and for nature, and cut open a whole apple and leave this for the 'Shee' the otherworldly guardian of this place.

Samhain

Samhain Introduction

This is the end of the old Celtic Year and on the day after Samhain the New Year begins, the Goddess of the Winter is awoken from her summer sleep and takes over the role of 'Mother' through the dark days of winter.

The Cailleach is well known as Hag of Winter here in the Celtic lands and many will know of her, but I want to make a point that she is not always a hag, she does not start off as 'old', but like all she gets older as the year goes on and depending on what she is doing. Here is a little piece I have written about her and perhaps you may want to take a deep breath, clear your head and come with me for a few moments.

The Lady Beara

Into a clearing in the woodland close to a loch comes a woman in her prime, dark, black hair hanging straight, deep, mystical blue eyes. She is wearing a long, dark blue dress, hung with the stars of a midnight sky at Samhain.

Although just awoken from her summer sleep she is mature with rounded breasts and motherly curved hips. Her name is Beara and she has been here since time began. Look at her face and you will see shapes, scroll patterns of deepest blue that appear as a moving tattoo. She smiles and holds out her hand and bids you fly with her over mountains, through valleys, greeting river spirits who rise up in welcome. She is full of love and shares it openly allowing you to sink blissfully into her warm, well-rounded breasts, where comfort and solace is abundant.

You see glimpses of her as she grows older as they appear like a changing scene. When older, her hair turned white and wavy as drifted snow, she brings with her the bleakness of winter, she will collect souls, bring frosts, snow and gales. But for now she is young, full red lipped, blue skinned and full of energy, which glistens like stars about her.

This is the Cailleach Bheur, but for now, we can greet her as Earth Mother, ancient one, The Lady Bheur.

This is the time to wake from her slumbers and in our group it has become a tradition that the Cailleach is woken up by tapping her hammer onto the ground. We are lucky enough to have a special wooden mallet shaped hammer with mystical symbols and feathers, which for us belongs to the Goddess. All through the summer she is wrapped up in silk and lace, sleeping sweetly until this time of year when we unwrap her during the ceremony and tap the hammer onto the ground, and it's from this point we would expect to have frosts, snow and all the storms of winter.

At this point, our dear Brigit will slip quietly into the background, perhaps to travel around to the other side of the world to enjoy spring all over again? Who can really say what our Deity does, no one has ever come back from the otherworld to let us know. Many different Goddesses have a similar tale, going down into the otherworld through the winter and then returning in the spring and many a Hag is known to wander this earth looking for souls to take with her to the next world.

We encourage our folks to come along to this festival dressed in their robes, and cloaks, even pointy hats. And we may bring along the last of the berry harvest, maybe a pumpkin? Or better still a 'neep' or turnip carved out hollow and ready for a candle in the middle.

Here is a Samhain Ceremony which includes the 'Waking of the Cailleach' which you can use of adapt for your own needs.

We take some time in this ceremony to remember our ancestors, those of our line, blood and place that have been called to the next life, especially in this last twelve months. We normally read aloud the names of those who have left us and for a moment keep silent in respect and in memory of their lives.

Parts of this ceremony were spoken from the heart on the day and not pre-written and so I will add some words which could be used but I must encourage you to write a little of your own or speak from the heart on the day.

Check list for the Samhain Ceremony
Money *(for the subs that you collect each time)*
Change of shoe (if necessary)
Mobile phone, always a good idea to keep in touch with travelers to the site.
Copy of the ceremony for each person
Wand or Staff
Samhain Incense with cauldron
Tongs to hold charcoal and spoon
Charcoal
Robes or Cloaks or seasonal dress
Small container to collect subs
First aid kit

Parts needed for the Samhain Ceremony
Elder 1
Elder 2
North
East
South
West
Horse
Eagle
Stag
Salmon
Raven
Call to the Cailleach Beara
Cailleach Beara
Maiden *(non speaking part)*
Reader of Poem

You will notice that there are more parts needed for the Samhain Ceremony, as there are for the Beltane Ceremony and you may need to double up if your group is small. We have found that if you are running an open group or you tend to invite many more folk along to the main well-known festivals, you do normally have enough people to take part. But read through the ceremony and you will soon see there are parts which can be removed, the poems perhaps and swapped for a chant of a song. If you have been using this little book from the start of the year, it is hoped that by now a larger and slightly more complicated ritual will come easily to you.

Samhain Ceremony

Opening Ceremony: (*Take the hand, which is offered you on your right, pull the energy through and give this energy to the person on your left by holding out your hand and linking with them.*)

(*Elder casts the Circle and then joins the Circle*)

Elder: (says *while all are holding hands*) Spirit of this place, we ask for your blessings, guidance and inspiration on this our Samhain ritual.

Elder 2: Let this ritual begin with peace for without peace no work can be done.

North: Let there be peace in the North.

East: Let there be peace in the East.

South: Let there be peace in the South.

West: Let there be peace in the West.

All: let there be peace throughout the world.

Elder 2: Let the Spirits of our Guardian Animals be called to this place.

Call to the Horse: (written by Potia)
We call to you
Great spirit of the Horse
Powerful steed of the northern plains
Loyal mount in the heat of battle
Strong as the white cut rock
Of the hollow hills
Thundering hoof
Drumbeat of the earth's heart
Lend us your wisdom
And steadfastness of purpose
We bid you
Hail and Welcome!

All: Hail and Welcome!

Call to the Eagle:
I call to the Eagle soaring above the cold mountain peaks,
With clear vision, swiftness and courage a fish is plucked effort-lessly from the loch.
With the spiritual power of the four directions and their sacred flow, the eagle shares knowledge and understanding as he feasts on his prey.
I ask you to join this rite and protect this sacred space.
I bid thee Hail and Welcome!

All: Hail and Welcome!

Call to the Stag:
I call to the Spirit of the majestic Stag in the heat of the rutting season,

He protects his herd on the frosty mornings, and misty autumn days.

As antlers flash through icy breath, and bodies tremble in ancient forces,

The forest resonates with your deep dark calls, as a reminder of life's continuity.

Spirit of stag, watch over us in our ceremony today. Hail and Welcome!

All: Hail and Welcome!

Call to the Salmon:
I stand in the West and call to the Spirit that pervades the Salmon.

Like the pristine clarity of mountain waters, we humbly invite you into our rite to bring definition and focus.

Imbue us with your vitality and your goodly qualities of fluidity, knowledge and wisdom.

And, like the Salmon who braves all obstacles, inspire us to be courageous when necessary.

Enter among us valiant Spirit.

We bid you, Hail and Welcome!

All: Hail and Welcome!

Elder 2: At this time, in the month of the Yew we mourn the death and loss of the God, sacrificed that all may live. We await his rebirth at Midwinter when the new Sun, the Child of Promise is reborn.

All: Blessings on those that sleep in the Summerlands, we remember them now.

Elder 2: Let our ancestors be called to this place, ancestors of blood, line and of place.

Elder: Call to the ancestors.

All: Hail and Welcome!

(In the center of the circle will be a bowl filled with fresh clean water, a candle, some nuts, acorns if possible, and an apple for each person present. Mead will be blessed during the ceremony, but on this occasion because of the death already of the corn God, there will be no bread, only apples and Mead!)

Raven: Call the Spirit of the Raven in your own words ... *the Raven with the knowledge of the Draoi (pronounced dree) Craft is called to this time and place. Once the Raven is called she (the Raven) will then call to the Cailleach!*

Call to the Cailleach Beara:
We call to you Lady of Winter. We call to you as you begin to wake from your summer's sleep. We call out to you mighty Cailleach. Awake! Awake from your dreaming. Awake and hear us! Join us; take up your hammer once more. Join us, be with us, and celebrate this time with us.

All Chant: Awake, awake, great Cailleach rise gently!

Words of the Cailleach:
This is my story. It is not the whole story, just a fragment that I am able now to speak.

I am old, older than you can imagine. Many have been my names and most are lost in the mists of time — even I cannot remember them all now. Today I am called the Hag of Winter, Queen Beara, the Veiled One, the Cailleach, the Carlin.

Most of you will think of me as the dark hag of winter and see me as a force belonging to the mountains of Scotland but I am much more than that.

I am the Mother of this Land known to you as Alba or Scotland. I am the Mother of all the Gods and Spirits waking and sleeping in its mountains and valleys. My hands dug out the lochs and my tears filled them. My feet created the valleys as I walked carrying my loads of earth and stone to make the hills and mountains. My breath formed the clouds that gather around those mountain peaks. My sweat fell down to create the streams of water flowing though the Land. I planted the first trees and tended them as I did the first of the animals to move into this land. Deer and cattle, goats, wolves and geese all these and more have I tended and loved.

You who call me hag and crone — you too would look haggard if you had lived as long as I.

You think me ugly? Is the midnight sky ugly? Are the stark mountains ugly? No, it is merely that I am different.

The tales tell of my skin being deep blue black, of my teeth with red stains, of my one eye like a deep pool and my tangled hair like the frost covered roots of Aspen. Do you know what that means?

Perhaps my skin is the darkness of the deepest caves; perhaps it is the midnight sky or the blackest of storm clouds over the sea. Is my hair the fall of hail in a storm or is it the milky stream of stars across the sky? Perhaps my one eye is the moon or perhaps it is the sea and the whirlpool of Corryvreckan is its centre. Perhaps my teeth are the cliffs of the coast or perhaps the red tinged clouds at sunset. I no longer know.

You think me harsh and cruel. I am a mother. Can any mother afford to always be loving and kind? Sometimes she must show she can be angered for her children to learn. Have those parents among you never had to discipline your children? Does that mean you no longer love them? No, of course not, you love them all the more.

I have been forgotten. I have been pushed into the form of the dark winter crone. My tales are those of winter and harshness but that it not all there is to me. I care more than you can imagine for this land and those that live upon it. I have mourned when my children have been torn from me. I have shrieked out my anger and pain in the storms. But I have danced too in joy at each new life born to me, sang in ecstasy when my children have returned to me. I weep with you in your loss and sing with you in your joy.

I speak now through the heart and mind of one of my children who has opened her heart to me. Listen to these words. Remember them. Remember me once more

Elder 2: We call to you, O Lord, the one who watches over the cycle of life and nature. You have been around from the beginning of the spring, when the first buds started to show, when the first blades of grass and the first snowdrops lifted their shy heads from underneath the white blanket of snow. It is almost winter now, and you are getting ready to lie down at the end of this cycle and rest, to be ready to rise up again in not a far time. We look up to you and see your wisdom, your power and your energy, we look at you and we see the strength of life. We call to you and bid you, Hail and Welcome!

All: Hail and welcome!

(All present now remember your loved ones who have gone to the Summerlands. Your much loved pets also and think about the past which you now must leave behind you in order to start a new year! Pause for a few moments, we will go around the circle in an anticlockwise direction to give everyone a chance to speak a name if they wish)

Elder speaks: In death, there is life, and at the end of life is death, for the wheel is always turning. As the dark times draw nigh, the light of life is only dimmed and it shall burst forth again. In the darkness when it is our time, we shall meet, and know and remember our loved ones again.

Elder 2: I bless this water, by the Salmon who swims in the rivers and lochs that we all know well! Spirit of Salmon, help us to see clearly what this next year holds for us all. This is the element of water!

(The Maiden takes the water bowl Sunwise to each person)

(The water can them be passed around for each to dip their fingers into and touch their forehead or simply to gaze into for a few seconds!)

Elder 2: *(holding the cup up in the air)* This is the cauldron of rebirth, let this mead be consecrated to life so that as we drink it we shall be renewed!

Elder: These apples have within them the seed of new life. I bless these apples and give the word of the Goddess that all who remember the continuing birth and rebirth throughout life and death, shall themselves be blessed. *(or words like this)*

(Pass the apples around the circle so all may take one, perhaps to eat tomorrow evening or if they wish to eat now.)

Song of Samhain *(taken from the Celtic Devotional by Caitlín Matthews.)*
I am the hallow-tide of all souls passing
I am the bright releaser of all pain
I am the quickener of the fallen seed
I am the glance of snow, the strike of rain
I am the hearth-fire and the welcome bread
I am the curtained awning of the pillow
I am unending wisdom's golden thread

Raven: *(Prayer for Soul's purpose taken from the Celtic Devotional by Caitlin Matthews.)*
Glad Giver, True Taker,
As the raven stoops upon decay and cleanses the earth,

So also do you take to yourself all scattered beings, keeping safe their souls.

In the mercy of your silence, we stand between life and death.

May the lifeblood in our veins bring us to perfect mindfulness of our soul's purpose.

Elder 2: (Samhain Prayer)
Dread Lord of Shadows, God of Life and giver of life —
Yet is the knowledge of thee, the knowledge of Death.
Open wide, I pray thee, the Gates through which all must pass.
Let our dear ones who have gone before
Return this night to make merry with us
And when our time comes, as it must,
O thou the Comforter, the Consoler, the Giver of Peace and Rest,
We will enter thy realms gladly and unafraid;
For we know that when rested and refreshed among our dear ones,
We will be reborn again by thy grace, and the grace of the Great Mother.
Let it be in the same place and the same time as our beloved ones,
And may we meet, and know, and remember, and love them again.

Horse: May the lands of Earth, Her forests, rivers, seas and all creatures upon Her be preserved and protected.

Eagle: May the world be filled with peace and light.

Stag: May the world be filled with radiance harmony and joy.

Salmon: May love pervade all those who seek to serve. May our souls be united thereby.

Elder 2: Let us thank the Spirit of the Raven for its presence at this rite today.

Raven: (*In your own words … The Spirit of the Raven will be thanked for the knowledge that he brings.*)

Elder 2: Let us thank the Goddess and our Ancestors for their presence here today.

Cailleach: (*Farewell to the Cailleach in your own words*).

Elder: (*Thanks to the Ancestors of Blood, Place and Spirit own words*)

Elder 2: May the spirits of the animals that we have called to this ceremony be thanked.

Farewell to the Horse: (*written by Potia*)
We thank you
Great spirit of the Horse
Powerful steed and loyal mount
Strength of the white cut rock
For giving us of your wisdom
And steadfastness of purpose
For combining our hearts
With the heart of the Earth
Stay if you will
Go if you must
We bid you
Hail and Farewell!

All: Hail and Farewell!

Farewell to the Eagle:

I call to give thanks to the spirit of the eagle,
    soaring above the cold mountain peaks sharing knowledge and understanding.

Thank you for attending our rite and guarding our sacred space.

Stay if you will but go if you must,

I bid you Hail and Farewell!

All: Hail and Farewell!

Farewell to the Stag:

Noble Spirit of Stag, Monarch of the herd,

We have honored your presence in our circle,

And we are touched by your gifts of vitality,

Power, and your regal qualities.

May your energy remain and protect us throughout the long winter months.

We thank you for spirit within our ritual today,

We bid you Hail and Farewell!

All: Hail and Farewell!

Farewell to the Salmon:

I, stand here to give thanks to the Spirit of the Salmon for being with us in this our Samhain rite.

For instilling within us the precious qualities of wisdom, knowledge, fluidity, and a respect for nature and each other.

For stimulating insight into understanding the mysteries of the cycle of our existences.

You have waved your hand across the deep pool of seeing, and have brought clarity and vision to us this day.

For this, we give our heartfelt thanks.

Go if you must … but stay if you will,

We bid you Hail and Farewell!

All: Hail and Farewell!

Elder 2: This celebration ends in peace as in peace it began. May the wealth of this rite and the blessings we have received go with us all as we depart this place, to nourish, strengthen and sustain us until we meet again.

Closing the Circle:
First, let everyone hold hands to form a complete circle.

(The Elder walks Widdershins and opens the Circle to the apparent world).

Chant: Let the circle be open yet unbroken, may the peace of the Goddess be always in our hearts, merry meet and merry part and merry meet again! *(Sung at least three times)*

Very Important … GROUP HUG

Midwinter Solstice and Yule

Midwinter Introduction

This is a wonderful time of the year, a very magical time when we watch carefully for the length of days after the longest night to see the sun grow in strength and the days start getting longer again.

At this moment, the Mother Goddess who struggles in labor all through that very long night gives birth to the Divine Child, the Sun. For three days and nights, this tiny baby collects his strength and soon by about the fourth day after the Midwinter, he starts to grow in strength and our days grow in length. This is the time we call 'Yule' when great celebrations are carried out all over the world, overtaken now by other spiritual paths with a frenzy of colored parcels, bells and that jolly, white bearded old man, dressed in red, with his 'ho, ho, ho'.

As Pagans, we do have some preparation to make as the Midwinter approaches and these are practical chores. It's always a good idea to have a clean and tidy up because it's likely we shall have visitors, and just as a mum to be will have a 'spring clean' and go about 'nesting', we need to do something like this ourselves in order to welcome the new Divine Child into our homes.

Sending seasonal greetings is one thing nearly all people do and Pagans are no exception, apart from the timing. I try very hard to have mine all done and posted so they arrive in time for the Midwinter. And more and more people are turning to 'e-cards' which can be timed to arrive on exactly the date you wish them to.

Food at this time of the year has always been very special, to give everyone a boost before the worst of the bad weather arrives in January. Having said that, I am writing this in late November 2010 and it has been snowing on and off now for several days, even here in the middle of the city of Glasgow in Scotland.

I am so glad there was a glut of berries in autumn and we were able to eat our fill, I should have known at that point that this winter was going to be a very cold one. But hopefully you have some berries saved in the form of jam or in your freezer, some to turn into a Midwinter pudding perhaps with ginger, nutmeg and all spice. Perhaps you are going to make a Yule Log or a Midwinter cake full of lots of fruit and spice. If not, and you live in a city, you can most likely buy a plain iced cake and put your own holly and ivy on it.

We like to take some seasonal 'cakes' or 'pies' to the Midwinter Ceremony and some mulled wine in place of our normal Mead and Oatcakes or bread. Standing in circle with a goblet of hot mulled wine, eating a mince pie, somehow you don't mind so much that it's freezing cold and perhaps even snowing.

I've made a note of what parts your will need for this ceremony and what else you need to take with you and it's perhaps a good idea to have this all sorted before the date, rather than stand around in the cold sorting out parts.

One more piece of advice, tell folk to dress up warmly and wear their winter boots, don't expect folk to arrive in their best ritual robes at this time of the year, its far better to be warm and dry! I know this sounds very silly, but if you live in a nice warm, centrally heated home, it's not easy to know just how cold it can be out in the woods, on a beach or in gardens at this time of the year.

Naturally, if you are a farmer or do some other out of doors work, you don't need this advice, but still, there could be some that do.

Checklist for the Midwinter Ceremony

One main candle and lots of little tea lights
Matches or a lighter
Incense, a cauldron and charcoal to burn the incense
Tongs to hold the charcoal while you light it and a spoon to add the incense over the burning charcoal
A chalice or goblet for the hot mulled wine

A plate or board with your chosen 'cakes'

A printed copy of the ceremony for everyone present

Perhaps some seasonal carols or songs and even musicians to help the tune along

A small container to collect 'subs', a small amount of money from each person to cover the costs of all the materials. This is something you should do at each festival in order to spread the burden of costs around.

Parts for the Ceremony

Elder One

Elder Two

East and Snow Goose

South and Stag

West and Seal

North and Fox

Spirit of Place

Ancestors

Young Winter God *(best called by a Mother figure)*

Mother Goddess *(best called by a Father figure)*

You will also need someone to take a light around the circle to all present to allow them to take their own little light.

It's also handy to have someone who will look after any incense you wish to burn and top it up during the ceremony.

Midwinter Solstice Ceremony

Elder 1: We have gathered together today to celebrate the shortest day, and the longest night. The midwinter solstice and a few days after this, Yuletide. Let us first cast a circle and make this place sacred for the ceremony today.

Elder 2: While I read this prayer, our Priestess will walk around the outside of this circle to cast a circle.

We cast our circle and by so doing we create a place of 'no time'.

This space is sacred, a holy place where the physical and non-physical come together.

Strengthen this place with your thoughts and intentions.

Make this circle a place of magic and mystery.

As the sacred wheel turns giving life to the seasons,

We who stand here today bear witness to the ever unfolding secrets.

We ask our deities to seal this circle with love, joy and security.

Blessed Be.

Elder 1: Now let us call to the direction, to the spirit animals and to the elements and ask that they join us today.

East: I call to the direction of the East, to the cold, crisp air, to the Snow Goose pure white as the driven snow. We ask the powers of the East to be with us today as we celebrate this Midwinter.

Welcome to the Snow Goose!

All: Welcome!

South: I call to the Midwinter Sun and to the powers of Fire in the South. To the Stag of the forest now guarding his herd, I ask you to be with us today in our ceremony.

Welcome to the Stag!

All: Welcome!

West: I call to the West, to the ever-flowing waters that fill our lakes and rivers. To the Seal who shelters in bays and along the western shore and I ask you to be with us now in our ceremony.

Welcome to the Seal!

All: Welcome!

North: I call to the North, to the solid foundation that is our Earth, its caves, hills and mountains. To the Fox who comes into our towns and cities, making dens in old graveyards. I ask you to stay with us and help guard us in our ceremony today.

Welcome to the Fox!

All: Welcome!

Spirit of Place: We call and ask that the guardian spirit of this place join us this day. You whose energy sweeps over this whole area, watching over us, protecting us. For a short while, stay with us as we celebrate this time of the year. Welcome!

All: Welcome Spirit of Place!

Ancestors: Ancestors of our family, of line, blood and contract. Those joined to us from many generations. I call to you now and ask that you join us, watch over us and stay with us for this ritual.

All: Welcome to our Ancestors!

Call to the Young Winter God:
I call to the new born Sun, the Divine Child of light and inspiration. We have waited all these dark days for you little one, and just when the days became so short and we felt that darkness would come all day long, you have been re-born. Your Blessed Mother gave birth to you on the longest night, all these hours of darkness she was in labor and now as the new day dawns, with it comes the light. The Sun is reborn, light and warmth will come once again and the Green Man of the Forest will grow stronger and stronger. Welcome to the newborn light. Welcome to the God!

All: Welcome Young God!

Call to the Mother Goddess:
Mother we call to you, we see your gentle touch and watch your silvery light make our nights clear. You have carried this new Divine Child for many months and on the longest night you labored to bring us a new Sun, a new light to bring us warmth. Come now and join us in our Midwinter celebration, inspire us and make us feel whole again.

Blessings on the Goddess who labors to bring us new light,

Blessings on the Goddess who will nourish this tiny child and in turn nourish us.

Blessings on She who was always there and will be there until time ceases to be.

Welcome Mother, Welcome Goddess!

All: Welcome to the Goddess!

Elder 1: We have met together today to mark the turning of the year, to celebrate the return of the Sun, of longer days and strong sunlight. To mark this time we are going to start in darkness and then light a single candle, from that all other candles will be lit.

(One single large candle is first lit and then from there each person will have the flame brought to them by the one chosen to be the light bearer for this occasion. She or He will walk around the circle taking the light to each person in turn. If there are a large number of people, those who have called to the four directions will step forward and light a smaller candle from the main light bearer, go back to their place and move around in a sunwise direction taking the light to all.)

Elder 2: This is a time when food for Mother Nature's children is very scarce, and it's also a time of giving gifts and of feasting and drinking. We are going to now offer little gifts to the birds and animals, tie a fat ball onto a tree, leave nuts and dried fruit out to be enjoyed by the creatures of the woodland and garden. Please will you bring your gifts into the centre of the circle now and once our ritual is over, we will all hang our things up on the tree or leave them close by.

(leave time now for all those who wish to bring gifts for the birds and animals to do so)

Elder 1: We will now bless and share the mulled wine and seasonal cakes for all to share.

(The two Elders, will now bless the wine and cakes and pass them around the group. At this time, we may have a carol to sing or some seasonal music played by some of our musicians.)

Elder 2: The light has come again, light has followed darkness and we rejoice in the birth of a new Divine Child. Now that the Wheel has turned once more, we have every confidence that the heat and strength of the Sun will grow stronger as the days also grow.

Elder 1: It is time now to say goodbye to all we have called to this time and place, to the animals, the spirit of place, to our patron Goddess and to the Mother Goddess with her Young Winter God.

Mother Goddess: We have been aware of your loving presence with us today and we want to thank you for staying with us. Your tender love enfolds us all in a warm embrace.

Blessings on you Mother, for all you have done for us on this longest night, we bid you a very fond Farewell!

All: Farewell Mother Goddess, Farewell!

Young Winter God: We now know that your tiny light has been reborn, as it is each year and we are so very pleased to have you with us once again. Small Divine Child, we treasure your reappearance once again and we will send you all our love as you grow strong and warm. Until we meet again in the spring, Farewell Young Winter God!

All: Farewell Young Winter God!

Ancestors: We speak with happy memories of our ancestors, those of you who danced, laughed and sang this new Sun into the World. Thank you for being here with us and until we meet up again in this special place, Farewell Ancestors!

All: Farewell Ancestors!

Spirit of Place: Guardian spirit of this special place, made holy for today's ceremony. We are always aware of the energy you spread around us and for this we want to say thank you! Farewell Spirit of Place!

All: Farewell Spirit of Place!

North: From the North, I want to thank the Fox who makes her bed in the old graveyards of this city, thank you for being with us today. Farewell Fox!

All: Farewell Fox!

West: From the every flowing waters of the West, I wish to thank the Seal for bringing such emotion and love to us this day. Farewell Seal!

All: Farewell Seal!

South: From the chill heat of the Midwinter Sun, I wish to thank the Stag for watching over us today. Farewell Stag!

All: Farewell Stag!

East: Flying over us from the cold East winds I want to thank the Snow Goose for being with us today in our ceremony. Farewell Snow Goose!

All: Farewell Snow Goose!

Elder 2: While I read the prayer to open our circle the Priestess will walk around the outside of the circle and dissolve the circle of energy which we created at the start of this ceremony, please stay in the circle until we have ended this rite.

Circle Opening Prayer:

As we bring our Ritual to a close and return to the apparent World, we remove the Magical Cloak that was our unseen Circle of Mystery.

And as 'no-time' becomes real time and the Worlds become one, we sense the Earth beneath our feet, the trees that surround us and the sky above our heads.

With those thoughts in mind push the energies within you down into the Earth and feel grounded.

May those who participated, seen and unseen in our ritual today leave this place in peace.

Elder1: The circle is open, but not broken, merry meet, merry part and merry meet again!

GROUP HUGIt is the custom of our own group for everyone in the circle to put their arms on the shoulders or around the person on both sides of them and make a few steps forward to have a group hug.

Part Two — Rites of Passage

Baby Naming Ceremonies

Baby Naming Ceremonies Introduction

There are people out in the general public who would very much like to have a baby naming with some spiritual content, but who are not members of any of the major religions and want something a little more than a civil ceremony. There are divided opinions as to making this kind of ceremony available to the general public, to those who would perhaps think of themselves as generally Pagan or Spiritual and those who have no special connection to any spiritual path at all. It is a very personal matter and one that only the Celebrant or Elder of a group can make their mind up about.

I would like to think that if someone brings a little baby to me and wants to have a naming ceremony, and I make it very clear that if I take the ceremony it will have some spiritual content and they are comfortable with that, then there is no reason to deny them this. The very fact that they have asked for it means to me that they have given this some thought, understood that they could in this country have a civil ceremony of naming and still want that extra spiritual content, then this is a good enough reason to conduct the ceremony.

Just that there are some Christian ministers who will not Christen a baby unless the parents are members of the Church, there will be others who would not turn anyone away if they come forward for this kind of service.

It is a good idea to go through a ceremony with the parents and ask them about their own beliefs before you book the ceremony. Some will say they love nature and are very keen on ecology and think this would be a very good idea. At this point it is perhaps worth digging a little deeper and finding out if they see the spirit of nature within all things?

There will be occasions when members of your own group have children and naturally come to you for a blessing on their babies, and this is when such a ceremony can be conducted within a regular gathering. As I write this, I am looking forward to holding a 'Faery Naming Ceremony' within the Spring Equinox, with the little siblings of the baby all coming along dressed as faeries.

It was the way of things in the days that our ancestors gathered together for the major festivals, sometimes not setting eyes on each other's families for six weeks at a time, so it would have been logical to presume that when they did all gather together, then the rites of passage would take place.

A new soul, a tiny child, ought to have the blessing from the elements, the Faery Folk, the Deity and Spirit that their family relates to, so it is a very good idea to walk around the circle with the baby in your arms, or in the arms of a parent or Goddess Parent and introduce them to each direction in turn. I have some different ceremonies to include in this chapter; the first is a 'Druidcraft' ritual, which can be held anywhere, inside or out. It is also something you can slot into one of the regular festival gatherings or even in an Esbat. We have also had the pleasure of conducting a baby naming as part of a Legal Handfasting, again it makes a very special day for all concerned.

Check list for items needed for a Baby Naming Ceremony
Map and directions to the venue
Mobile phone
Compass or application for your smart phone to find the directions
Copy of the ceremony for each person
Perhaps white rose petals to cast a circle
Wand
Incense, but check with parents if this is acceptable
Cauldron, charcoal, tongs and spoon

*A small bottle of blended essential oils to bless the baby
A certificate to sign and give the family after the ceremony.

*Please be aware that many essential oils are not suitable for babies, but Lavender or Rose can be used diluted into natural carrier oil. You should blend the oil before hand, bless and consecrate it in your own home or temple surroundings. Wrap the bottle up in a piece of natural material if possible and then it is a very nice idea to give the parents this blend as a gift, they can add a little into the babies bath water for a few days after the ceremony.

Parts needed for a Druidcraft Baby Naming
You may need to share the major parts with your working partner or even do them all you self, it's very daunting to expect folks who have never done anything like this before to read a part.
2 Elders or Celebrants, this ceremony has, HP/High Priest and HPS/High Priestess
Baby
Parents or Parent
Goddess Parents
If possible the Grandparents
Four people to hold up symbols for the elements

A Druidcraft Naming Ceremony
A Pagan Ceremony or Ritual is not held in a permanent place, it's usually held out of doors and the area will be made special and sacred for this time.

Before we begin the Celebrants will talk to everyone present and explain what is going to take place, they will bless and consecrate the area chosen for the Ceremony.

Welcome
The parents will be asked to introduce themselves, i.e. to say who they are and whom they have with them.

We will ask if they wish their child to be shown to the four quarters and named in the circle and the parents would answer.

The Opening Ceremony

This is exactly like any of the ceremonies, which have four directions, so it's possible to choose the type of ceremony that would appeal to the parents.

HP: Now that we are all here, let us call to the elements, to the Goddess and the God, and to our ancestors, so that they and all of us can witness this rite.

(HPS *walks slowly to the East, and the HP to the West, they then call to the quarters, the HPS will call to the East and the South and the HP to the West and the North. At each quarter the person with that element holds is up for all to see.*)

HPS East: We call to the East to the element of Air, to the Sky at dawn, to the pure clear air at the rising of the Sun, may the powers of the East be with us. We bid you Hail and Welcome!

All: Hail and Welcome!

HPS South: We call to the South to the element of Fire, to the Sun at noon radiating its warmth and light, may the powers of the South be with us. We bid you Hail and Welcome!

All: Hail and Welcome!

HP West: We call to the West to the element of Water, to the silvery Moon rising at sunset to bring depth to our emotions, may the powers of the West be with us. We bid you Hail and Welcome!

All: Hail and Welcome!

HP North: We call to the North to the element of Earth, to the Northern lights and the glittering stars at midnight, we call to the deep, abiding and fruitful earth, may the powers of the North be with us. We bid you Hail and Welcome!

All: Hail and Welcome!

HPS: A Call to the Lady
We ask you to be with us Lady, you have been called by many different names in many ages of men.

Maid, fresh from childhood, innocent girl bring your fresh young eyes and help us look at things from your viewpoint.

Mother, blooming and full of life,

Nourish us with your loving care.

Wise women, elder with such a long passage of time behind you.

Give us wisdom to understand the new steps we take now.

From seed and bud, from root and branch,

As the leaves open, as they grow and blossom,

As they darken, wither and die,

As the wheel turns and the cycle continues,

Come to us Lady, touch us, fill us,

Open our minds and eyes, let our ears hear.

Hail Lady and Welcome!

All: Hail and Welcome!

HP: A Call to the Lord
Welcome among us Lord! You who are known by so many names, from so many walks of life and time.

Young man, bring your energy and strength to us today,

Lover and consort, we call to you,

Fill our bodies with your life giving magic.

Wise man, soul friend, on whom we lean and turn to for advice,

Open our eyes that we can see and understand.
From seed to bud, from root to branch,
Bring us life, strength and wisdom,
Stand with us as the wheel of the year turns,
Strengthen us now as we take new steps forward.
Come among us Lord, fire us with your energy,
Hail Lord and Welcome!

All: Hail and Welcome!

HPS: A Call to Our Ancestors

We call to our ancestors of line and blood, those who have gone before us, those who have lived and worked in this city many years before. In particular, I call to .... (name) and ask that you join us today to witness this rite.

I call also to ...., (name) who went to the Summerlands in our living memory, I ask that you join us to witness this rite. And to all of you I bid, Hail and Welcome!

All: Hail and Welcome!

HP: A Call to the Spirit of Place, Clutha

Clutha, you are the spirit of this dear green place and of its valley and river running out to the sea. We see you all around in the life and strength of the very essence of the city. I ask you now to join us and watch over us as we hold this ceremony. Clutha, I bid you, Hail and Welcome!

All: Hail and Welcome!

HPS: All are now called and gathered to witness this ceremony, let us begin.

The Naming Ceremony

HP: Will you bring baby .... (name) into the centre of the circle please.

HPS: We are now going to walk baby to the four quarters and ask that the elements acknowledge this small person. (*Walks to the East with the baby, if this is not possible we would ask the parents or Goddess parents to walk with us holding the baby*)

HP: Guardians of Air, Faery Sylphs from the East, this is .... (name of baby) the daughter of .... (name of parents) may your fresh clean air always fill her with the breath of this life. We call for a blessing of the element of Air, to mote it be!

All: So mote it be!

(Walks to the South and then West and lastly North)

HPS: Guardians of Fire, Faery Salamanders from the South, this is .... (name) the daughter of .... (name). May the warmth of the Sun always bring strength and energy to her and we call for a blessing of the element of Fire, so mote it be!

All: So mote it be!

HP: Guardians of Water, Faery Undines from the West, this is .... (name), the daughter of ....(name). May the gentle water wash her troubles away and bring her peace, we call for a blessing of the element of Water, to mote it be!

All: So mote it be!

HPS: Guardians of Earth, Faery Gnomes from the North, this is

.... (name), the daughter of .... (name). May the stability of the Earth always bring her security, we call for a blessing of the element of Earth, so mote it be!

All: So mote it be!

(The child is then brought into the center of the circle and the Celebrants will call for a blessing of the Goddess and God on the baby and will anoint her forehead with blessed and consecrated oil.)

(If there are Goddess Parents they will be asked to make a promise to all present that they will watch and support this child. If there are any other traditions which are requested, this would be a good time to hold them.)

Sharing of Bread and Mead *(The Sacred meal)*

HPS: At this stage of our ceremony, we are going to share bread and mead with everyone present. While we do this, our wish for this child and her family is that they will never hunger nor thirst in this life.

(At this point Mead and Bread can be blessed and shared. If this is done we will consecrate the Mead and Bread and then the HP will offer the cup to the HPS who will take some and hand it back to the HP. He will then give the chalice to the parents who will take a sip and then offer the chalice back. As the chalice is passed from HP to Mother and then from Mother to Father the words, 'Blessed Be' shall be said quietly and a light kiss exchanged.

The bread or cakes will then be consecrated, this time the cakes will be offered to the HP who will take some and offer them to the HPS. She will then turn to the parents and offer the cakes to them, they will take some and then offer the cakes or bread to the celebrants. The Goddess parents can then be offered the mead and cake and, finally it can be offered out to all present

The Closing Ceremony

HPS: We have now come to the time in our ceremony to say goodbye or bid farewell to all those how have been called to this time and place.

HP: Farewell to Clutha

Clutha, spirit of this beautiful place we want to thank you for being with us today, go if you must but stay if you will, I bid you Hail and Farewell!

All: Hail and Farewell!

HPS: Farewell to the Ancestors

Ancestors of our line and blood, those of you who walked this Earth before us, we thank you for being here with us today from your beautiful realm. We ask your blessing on this family today and we give you in return our love, a blessing on you, we know you are only a thought away and we thank you for being here with us. Go, all of you, if you must but stay if you will, I bid you Hail and Farewell!

All: Hail and Farewell!

HP: Farewell to the Lord

A blessing on you Lord,
You have filled us with vital life,
Your arms hold us and strengthen us,
You came to us when we needed you most,
Go if you must, but stay if you will,
Hail Lord and Farewell!

All: Hail and Farewell!

HPS: Farewell to the Lady

A blessing on you Lady,
You have loved us and nourished us,
We feel your gentle caress; your peace surrounds us,
You saw us from the spirit realm,
Go if you must, but stay if you will,
Hail Lady and Farewell!

All: Hail and Farewell!

(The Celebrants now walk to the North and South, the HPS bids farewell to the North and to the West. The HP bids farewell to the South and the East.)

HPS North: I call to the North, to the Element of Earth, thank you for being here with us today, and I bid you Hail and Farewell!

All: Hail and Farewell!

HPS West: I call to the West, to the Element of Water, thank you for being with us here today, and I bid you Hail and Farewell!

HP South: I call to the South, to the element of Fire, to the noonday Sun with its warmth, I think you for being here with us today, and I bid you Hail and Farewell!

All: Hail and Farewell!

HP East: I call to the East, to the Element of Air, for inspiration and clarity of thought I thank you, and for being with us today, I bid you Hail and Farewell!

All: Hail and Farewell!

Closing the Circle(*The HP will read the words for closing the Druid Circle from a card while the HPS will take a wand and walk around the outside of everyone present.*)

HPS: The circle is open, yet unbroken!

All: Merry meet and merry part and merry meet again!

Once the Circle is open, everyone is welcome to take photos and we are happy to pose again and go over parts of the ceremony to let everyone take photos.

Wiccan Baby Naming Ceremony
(To be held during a regular Esbat Ceremony)

Open the Esbat in the normal manner and when it comes to closing down, do this in the normal manner your Coven uses. Once the opening ceremony is complete, conduct this ceremony in the centre of the ritual.

HP: Lord, guide .... (name) in the ways of kindness and courage. Let her be valiant and wise, as you are. Give to her your talents and appreciation for poetry, art and music. Warm her through the long days of learning ahead.

HPS: Lady, protect .... (name) with your vigilance, let her breathe in your fresh air of the forest. Let her be strong, free and independent as you are. Guide her hunt for her own path. Protect her through the darkest of nights, and help her ponder the infinity of the starry sky.

(One of the parents takes baby and faces her once in each direction, starting with east.)

(Once HPS has made the blessing for that direction, they walk slowly

clockwise until they face the next direction, where they pause for the next statement.)

High Priest: Elements of the East! Recognize this small person .... (name). Help her to soar in the limitless sky of thought and imagination. Send .... (name) gentle breezes to guide her on her path. Bless .... (name) with all the airborne powers of the East. So Mote it be!

All: So mote it be!

HPS 2: Elements of the South! Recognize this small person .... (name). Warm her, strengthen her Will with your energy. Send .... (name) light to help her prevail in the challenges that await her. Bless .... (name) with all the burning powers of the South. So mote it be!

All: So mote it be!

HPS 3: Elements of the West! Recognize this small person .... (name). Help her to swim the deep seas of emotion and empathy. Send .... (name) cleansing waters to cleanse her of doubts and confusion. Bless .... (name) with all the flowing powers of the West. So mote it be!

All: So mote it be!

HPS 1: Elements of the North! Recognize this small person .... (name), help her to stand firm on mother earth. Send .... (name) rich soil to root in, and connect her with all that is. Bless (name) with all the solid powers of the North. So mote it be!

All: So mote it be!

Optional Goddess Parent/Coven Component

(The Goddess Parents or Group/Grove/Coven should be brought forth then to the centre of the circle, and the parent as well. The parent should hold the baby.)

HP: In times past, children were not the sole responsibility of the biological parents. This responsibility is too great for any one or two people to bear alone. I hope that all in the community would help a child in need. As a reminder that children need many sources of support, the tradition of the god/goddess parents arose. These chosen people here tonight will have a special relationship with .... will be there should she need someone outside the home to talk to. To share experiences, and to be a neutral and loving third party should the family need help.

Parents: Goddess Parent/group, will you participate in the growing years of this child, ...Through your connection with this group, will you be there to listen to her, and help and advise us for her welfare if necessary?

Goddess parents/Group answer:

(The Parent passes the child to the Goddess parent/Group. If there is more than one, the goddess parent holding the child repeats the statement and then hands the baby to the other or next godparent. Then the parent takes the child back and says: the statement)

Goddess parents and parent: Bless and keep you .... I will be here for you.

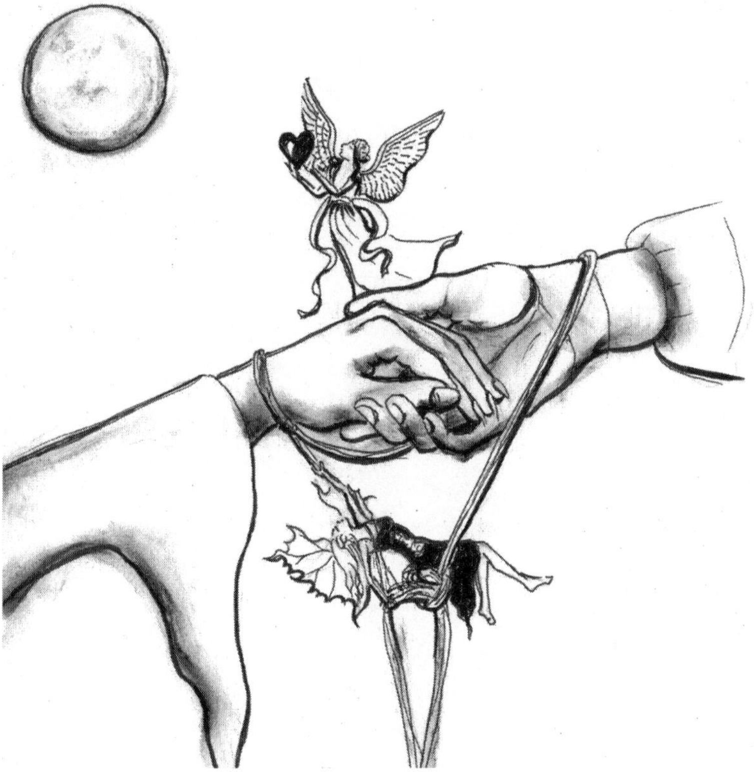

Handfasting Ceremonies

Handfasting Ceremonies or Pagan and Heathen Marriage
Introduction

I am one of a growing number of Celebrants who are authorized in Scotland to conduct Legal Handfasting Ceremonies or Pagan Marriages and have been for several years now. My husband and working partner and I have been conducting rites of passage for some time and happily now we can do these legally for folk.

Many couples put off getting married for different reasons and one of them is the cost, the other is that one partner comes from a different original spiritual path and their families are still worshiping within these faiths. We all understand what a stress this can be, when parents of the bride want a 'White Wedding' in their church and parents of the bridegroom would not even venture into that church, because all through generations their family have been of a different faith or just a different denomination.

We have conducted marriage ceremonies for couples where this has been the main reason for asking us to take their ceremony. It is not the best idea at all and there have been the occasional time when I have pointed out that perhaps it would be better to have a civil ceremony. But if the couple can convince me that they are Pagan or Heathen themselves, have been for some time and really do want a marriage ceremony, perhaps out of doors, maybe at an ancient site, then naturally we will do all we can to help them achieve this goal. Not that I would refuse an indoor ceremony and we have done several of these.

My personal opinion is that a Wedding or Marriage should not cost the earth at all, so many pay thousands and thousands for their ceremony, reception and all the trimmings that go with this, when it can be done for under one thousand pounds. Even less, it can cost as little as three or four hundred pounds, and that's counting the cost of clothes, stationary, Celebrants fees, and a meal or reception after the ceremony.

Not all Celebrants have a set charge, some work full time and earn a good wage and when they do the occasional ceremony will do so for just the cost of their travel to and from the event, which just leaves the couple with the costs of the legal paperwork that has to be paid for.

I actually spend hours and hours writing and planning a marriage ceremony and although I do have a couple of 'samples' which I will give you here, it still requires a few hours to alter a ceremony, add some suitable graphics, format and print out copies for everyone taking an active role. Most of the time it's a case of starting from scratch and writing something which the couple have requested, all of which takes time. So, for all of this I do charge a fee and most Celebrants will do the same.

What I do not charge for is my time and my 'service', we do not charge for any meetings prior to the event and we do not take into consideration any amount of time needed. I believe that the service I can offer is very much like magic and healing, it cannot be brought, it is given.

So the choice of what kind of Pagan or Heathen ceremony you would like for your marriage is very much up to you, if you come to me, we will go through a list of questions with you to find what would perhaps suit you and what you especially would like to include. Broomstick? To jump or not to jump? Almost all couples will ask if they jump the broomstick during the ceremony and we are only too happy to include this tradition. But let's look a little at the meaning behind all of this.

The old saying of 'Living Over the Broom' is a well known saying for couples who are not legally married or different reasons, normally these days because one of them is waiting for a divorce from a previous partnership to come through. And some who just do not feel it is necessary to have an official ceremony. But in days gone by, especially in very isolated areas a couple would simply tell their friends and family that they were going to live together as a couple and maybe have a little ceremony when the family would actually hold out a broom and they would jump it together and that was good enough for many. They had no Vicar, no Druid or other figure of authority and would simply want to get on with life until such time as it was possible to have a formal ceremony. Some never even bothered and others would eventually have a Wedding and baptize all the children at the same time.

The 'Broom' in Paganism, and in a Marriage is a symbol of fertility, especially of the Lord of the Forest, the Pagan God. In jumping a Pagan Broomstick during the ceremony, the couple is asking for fertility. This can be a literal thing or it can be fertility of mind or artistic creativity. It has its serious side and it is also great fun and a very old tradition which most are happy with.

There is also a thought that you would sweep out the old and sweep in the new but this may come from a misunderstanding about its uses at Samhain or even at regular meetings when we would go round an area and make the area safe, pick up fallen branches and literally, sweep the area. Perhaps you would disagree with this and I have to add that this is my own understanding and personal opinion, which I have reached after years of practice.

Our broomstick that we take along to Handfasting Ceremonies is a large one, decorated with ribbons and bows, I hold one end and my partner holds the other end off the ground and we get the couple to jump with their wrists still bound.

We often get requests to offer this to other couples as well during a Handfasting, many times these are couples who have been trying to start a family for some time without any luck and feel the magic of the occasion will help. If you feel it will help, if the couple in question think it will help and if there is no medical reason to prevent them starting a family, then it's a good idea to jump. Often the magic in positive thought and prayer goes a long way towards helping in many ways. We are very happy to allow others to jump the broomstick at a Handfastingif this is something the bride and groom would like as well.

At Beltane, we nearly always conduct a ceremony where the May Queen and the May King will jump the broomstick and we would then offer this to any other couple who has come along to the ceremony. But a warning! Over the last few years, babies have been born nine months after the May Queen and King took on these roles! Only twice in the last few years has this been the case and it is possible that the couples in question may have had medical reasons to prevent their own fertility, or it is even possible that the couple only took on these roles for the day and were not in fact partners in life.

I have three different Handfasting Ceremonies to share with you, the first is a Druidcraft ritual and the second is a Celtic ritual. The third is a very short ceremony, which can be used for a Legal Marriage when perhaps a ceremony has already taken place, maybe in an area close to the family of the couple and for their own reasons a Pagan Spiritual Legal short ritual is very much what the couple would like.

There is always the occasion when some of the official paperwork does not arrive in time, everything is booked and paid for, all the travel arrangements are made and a problem occurs in the last few days. We would always go ahead with the main ceremony and then soon after, once the official paperwork arrives, we can conduct this short ceremony and then sign the official paperwork for the couple. It is worth adding that if this happens to you, we would still require two witnesses to sign a legal marriage certificate. We may be able to find a couple of members of our local Druidcraft group to come along and do this for you, but you would be expected to pay their bus fares and maybe buy them a cup of tea or a drink afterwards.

Check List for a Druidcraft Handfasting
Map & money
Satellite Navigation with address in

Mobile phones

Full Scripts x 10

Order of ceremony for all guests

Fountain pen with permanent black ink filled chamber, to sign the legal paperwork

Handfasting Wand

Candles for 4 quarters (coloured votive)

Candle lighter and matches

Main Handfasting Candle and Candle holder

Incense

Charcoal with cauldron

Tongs to hold charcoal

Spoon for the incense

Belt

Chalice

Athame

Oatcakes or bread

Mead

Baskets for oatcakes

Handfasting cords

Robe and cloak for Celebrant if required

Laminated vows

Laminated Blessing

Laminated opening and closing prayer

Broomstick

First aid kit

Official paperwork — Schedule

Handfasting Certificate if requested

Business Cards

Parts needed for a Druidcraft Handfasting

Celebrants

Bride and Groom

Best man and Bridesmaid

Four family members or friends to hold votive candles as follows
East
South
West
North
Music — someone to either sing a song or play some music or perhaps a piper?

The list of people to take part in your Handfasting is very much up to you. It may be possible for you to find friends or family to take a much more active part and you may have someone you want to sing a song or play some music. It may be that you choose to have a ceremony that is very personal to you and you don't wish to have any other guests apart from the two legal witnesses.

A Legal Druidcraft Handfasting

A Pagan Ceremony or Ritual is not held in a permanent place, it's usually held out of doors and the area will be made special and sacred for this time.

Before we begin the Celebrants will talk to everyone present and explain what is going to take place, they will bless and consecrate the area chosen for the Handfasting Ceremony with water and with incense.

Welcoming the Wedding Party

HP: (*speaks to the bridesmaid*) Greetings, will you tell me who you are and whom do you bring with you?

Bridesmaid: My name is .... and I bring with me .... who wishes to come before the Goddess and the God to be Handfasted this day!

HP: Come closer into this circle, *(waits while they come closer)* …………, do you come here of your own free will?

Bride: I do!

HP: Welcome to you both!

HPS: *(speaks to the best man)* Greetings, can you tell me who you are and whom do you bring with you this day?

Best man: My name is …………, and I bring with me ………… who wishes to come before the Goddess and the God to be Handfasted this day!

HPS: Come closer into this circle, *(waits while they come closer)* …………, do you come here of your own free will?

Bridegroom: I do!

HPS: Welcome to you both!

The Opening Ceremony

HP: Now that we are all here, let us call to the elements, to the Goddess and the God, and to our ancestors, so that they, and all of us can witness this rite.

(HPS walks slowly to the East, and the HP to the West, they then call to the quarters, the HPS will call to the East and the South and the HP to the West and the North.

At each quarter the person with that element holds is up for all to see.)

HPS East: We call to the East to the element of Air, to the Sky at dawn, to the hawk soaring in the pure clear air at the rising of the Sun, may the powers of the East be with us. We bid you Hail and

Welcome!

All: Hail and Welcome!

HPS South: We call to the South to the element of Fire, to the Sun at noon radiating its warmth and light, to the great stag in the heat of the chase, may the powers of the South be with us. We bid you Hail and Welcome!

All: Hail and Welcome!

HP West: We call to the West to the element of Water, to the silvery Moon rising at sunset to bring depth to our emotions, to the salmon of wisdom who dwells in the sacred waters of the pool, may the powers of the West be with us. We bid you Hail and Welcome!

All: Hail and Welcome!

HP North: We call to the North to the element of Earth, to the Northern lights and the glittering stars at midnight, to the great bear of the starry heavens, we call to the deep, abiding and fruitful earth, may the powers of the North be with us. We bid you Hail and Welcome!

All: Hail and Welcome!

HPS: A Call to the Lady
We ask you to be with us Lady, you have been called by many different names in many ages of men.

Maid, fresh from childhood, innocent girl bring your fresh young eyes and help us look at things from your viewpoint.

Mother, blooming and full of life,

Nourish us with your loving care.

Wise women, elder with such a long passage of time behind

you.

Give us wisdom to understand the new steps we take now.
From seed and bud, from root and branch,
As the leaves open, as they grow and blossom,
As they darken, wither and die,
As the wheel turns and the cycle continues,
Come to us Lady, touch us, fill us,
Open our minds and eyes, let our ears hear.
Hail Lady and Welcome!

All: Hail and Welcome!

HP: A Call to the Lord

Welcome among us Lord! You who are known by so many names, from so many walks of life and time.
Young man, bring your energy and strength to us today,
Lover and consort, we call to you,
Fill our bodies with your life giving magic.
Wise man, soul friend, on whom we lean and turn to for advice,
Open our eyes that we can see and understand.
From seed to bud, from root to branch,
Bring us life, strength and wisdom,
Stand with us as the wheel of the year turns,
Strengthen us now as we take new steps forward.
Come among us Lord, fire us with your energy,
Hail Lord and Welcome!

All: Hail and Welcome!

HPS: A Call to Our Ancestors

We call to our ancestors of line and blood, those who have gone before us, those who have lived and worked in this city many years before. In particular, I call to .... and ask that you join us today to witness this rite.

I call also to ...., who went to the Summerlands in our living memory, I ask that you join us to witness this rite. And to all of you I bid, Hail and Welcome!

All: Hail and Welcome!

HP: A Call to the Spirit of Place, Clutha
Clutha, you are the spirit of this dear green place and of its valley and river running out to the sea. We see you all around in the life and strength of the very essence of the city. I ask you now to join us and watch over us as we hold this Handfasting ceremony. Clutha, I bid you, Hail and Welcome!

All: Hail and Welcome!

HPS: All are now called and gathered to witness this ceremony, let us begin.

The Handfasting
(The bride and groom now come to the centre of the circle, close to the Alter or table and face each other)

HP: ...., please turn to face your future husband, *(steps up to the Bride and reads...)*
O women, behold thy chosen man and gaze upon his beauty. Thou must know that he is made in the image of the God, strong and upright, the protector of the weak, who shall be thy loyal soul mate. See in his manhood the sword of power from which flows the very force that gives us life. Rejoice in the strength of his embrace and be whole!

HPS: ...., please continue to face your future wife, *(steps up to the bridegroom and reads...)*
O man, behold thy chosen women and gaze upon her beauty.

Thou must know that she is made in the image of the goddess, glorious and beautiful, strong and wise, priestess and mother. See in her thy fulfillment in love and companionship. See in her thy inner feminine self and rejoice that in her thou mayest find fulfillment. See in her womanhood the grail of immortality, the sacred cauldron that is the very cradle of life itself.

HP: Can we now have the rings? *(Best man gives the rings to the celebrants who will bless them together.)* A ring is a ...

The Vows

HPS: Can I ask you now to read your vows to each other. *(The HPS gives the prepared vows to each, which have been previously placed on the altar).*

I .... declare that I take you ...., to be my lawful husband.

You are the one I have chosen to spend the rest of my life with,
I love and trust you without question.

You are the one I want to see when I first open my eyes in the morning,

And it is you that I want to give my last kiss of each night to.

I will always make every effort to be at your side whenever you need me.

As the Sun lights each day, and the Moon lights the night,

I will be there for you throughout our Springs, Summers, Autumns and Winters.

And death shall not part us; for in the fullness of time,

once more we shall be born again at the same time and in the same place as

each other;

and will know, and remember, to love again, throughout eternity.

I, ... declare that I take you, ..., to be my lawful Wife.

You are the one I have chosen to spend the rest of my life with,

I love and trust you without question.

You are the one I want to see when I first open my eyes from sleep,

And it is you that I want to give my last kiss to before I fall asleep.

I am the one who will support and protect you.

I will make every effort to be there for you, whenever you need me.

As the Sun lights each day, and the Moon lights the night,

I will be there for you throughout our Springs, Summers, Autumns and Winters.

And death shall not part us; for in the fullness of time,

once more we shall be born again at the same time and in the same place as

each other;

and will know, and remember, to love again, throughout eternity.

HPS: .... and .... will you now give each other the rings you have brought for this ceremony.

(The couple place the rings on each other's wedding finger, and then turn to hold the hand they wish to be bound, one to the other. The Celebrants place the Handfasting cords over the top of their joined hands and say ...)

HP: Let the Sun and the Lord bear witness that these two persons wish to be bound to each other! *(winds the golden cord around their wrists)*

HP: Let the Moon and the Lady bear witness that these two persons wish to be bound to each other! *(winds the silver cord around their wrists)*

Sponsors: Let the Earth our Mother, and all here present bear witness that .... and .... wish to be bound to each other!

HPS: May all those here present bear witness that you are now bound together and .... and ...., I now declare you husband and wife and may your union be blessed! *(Applause now!)*

(The couple hold their hands up high so all can see, we cheer and applaud. Once everyone has seen the bound hands, the groom slips the cord off their hands and ties it around the waist of his bride.)

Sharing of Bread and Mead: *The Sacred meal!*

HPS: At this stage of our ceremony, we are going to share bread and mead with the new married couple. While we do this, our wish for .... and .... is that they will never hunger nor thirst in their married life together.

(At this point Mead and Bread can be blessed and shared, if this is done we will consecrate the Mead and Bread and then the HP will offer the cup to the HPS who will take some and hand it back to the HP. He will then give the chalice to the Bride who will take a sip and then offer the chalice to her Groom. As the chalice is passed from HP to Bride and then from Bride to Bridegroom the words, 'Blessed Be' shall be said quietly and a light kiss exchanged.

The bread or cakes will then be consecrated, this time the cakes will be offered to the HP who will take some and offer them to the HPS. She will then turn to the Groom and offer the cakes to him, he will take some and then offer the cakes or bread to his Bride. The bridesmaid and the best man can then be offered the mead and cakes, then it can be offered out to all present.)

The Blessing, read by the High Priest

Native American Indian Wedding Blessing

Now you will feel no rain, for each will shelter the other.
Now you will feel no cold, for each will warm the other.
Now you will feel no solitude for each will company the other.
Now you are two persons, but both will lead one life.
Go now to your dwelling place to begin the days of your life together,
And may your days be good and long upon the Earth.
And in another time and place,
May you meet again, know and love again,
Throughout Eternity.
Author unknown

The Closing Ceremony

HPS: We have now come to the time in our ceremony to say goodbye or bid farewell to all those how have been called to this time and place.

HP: Farewell to Clutha

Clutha, spirit of this beautiful place we want to thank you for being with us today, go if you must but stay if you will, I bid you Hail and Farewell!

All: Hail and Farewell!

HPS: Farewell to the Ancestors

Ancestors of our line and blood, those of you who walked this Earth before us, we thank you for being here with us today from your beautiful realm .... We ask your blessing on this couple today and we give you in return our love ...., a blessing on you, we know you are only a thought away and we thank you for being here with us. Go, all of you, if you must but stay if you will, I bid you Hail and Farewell!

All: Hail and Farewell!

HP: Farewell to the Lord
A blessing on you Lord,
You have filled us with vital life,
Your arms hold us and strengthen us,
You came to us when we needed you most,
Go if you must, but stay if you will,
Hail Lord and Farewell!

All: Hail and Farewell!

HPS: Farewell to the Lady
A blessing on you Lady,
You have loved us and nourished us,
We feel your gentle caress; your peace surrounds us,
You saw us from the spirit realm,
Go if you must, but stay if you will,
Hail Lady and Farewell!

All: Hail and Farewell!

(The Celebrants now walk to the North and South, the HPS bids farewell to the North and to the West. The HP bids farewell to the South and the East.)

HPS North: I call to the North, to the Element of Earth to Great Bear of the starry heavens, thank you for being here with us today, and I bid you Hail and Farewell!

All: Hail and Farewell!

HPS West: I call to the West, to the Element of Water, to the Salmon of Wisdom who swims in the deep lochs and rivers, thank you for being with us here today, and I bid you Hail and Farewell!

All: Hail and Farewell!

HP South: I call to the South, to the element of Fire, To the Stag of the Forest, full of passion and to the noonday Sun with its warmth, I thank you for being here with us today, and I bid you Hail and Farewell!

All: Hail and Farewell!

HP East: I call to the East, to the Element of Air, to the Hawk circling in the high currents of a clear blue sky, for inspiration and clarity of thought I thank you for being with us today and I bid you Hail and Farewell!

All: Hail and Farewell!

Closing the Circle

(The HP will read the words for closing the Druid Circle from a card while the HPS will take a wand and walk around the outside of everyone present)

HPS: The circle is open, yet unbroken!

All: Merry meet and merry part and merry meet again!

(Once the Circle is open, everyone is welcome to take photos and we are happy to pose again and go over parts of the ceremony to let everyone take photos.)

A Celtic Handfasting
The area will be cleansed at the start, perhaps before the guests arrive. The altar is laid out and the candles made ready.

A word to everyone at the start of the ceremony to explain what is going to happen today.

The guests will come into the area between two incense cauldrons/fires, which will be attended by two men.

Once all the guests are either seated or standing in place we will ask the Groom and his sponsor to come towards the circle (the sponsors and the bride and groom will speak clearly, so all present can hear their answers)

HPS: Who are you and why do you come to this circle today?

Groom's Sponsor: I am .... and I come bringing with me .... who wishes to be Handfasted this day.

HPS: *(Groom)* ...., have you come here of your own free will?

Groom: I have!

HP: (Speaking to Bride's Sponsor) Will you tell us please, who are you and who do you bring with you this day?

Bride's Sponsor: I am .... and I bring with me .... who wishes to be Handfasted this day.

HPS: *(Bride)* ...., have you come here of your own free will?

Bride: I have!

Celebrants: We welcome you into this circle today.

(The wedding party now come into the circle and stand in the middle, opposite the two celebrants).

Casting the Circle

(While the HP reads the words of the circle casting prayer, the HPS will walk around the outside of all gathered and with a wand, cast a circle.)

HP: (words of casting prayer)

(Taking a lighting stick with them, the HPS and HP will go to stand in place to call the three Celtic Realms as they get to each area they will light the votive candle and call to the Earth, Sea and Sky.)

Calling the Realms

HP: Earth — Lighting the Votive Candle

I am the earth under your feet

The solid ground into which you build your foundations

I am the dark earth, which supports this special place.

Give me your seeds, I will nourish your roots and help your plants to bear fruit.

I am under your feet and I will help you stand firm!

HPS: Sky — Lighting the Sky Votive Candle

I am the vault of heaven, the atmosphere always above this beautiful place.

It is through and above me that the wind blows,

Through me, the gentle summer breeze brings fresh clean air to this space,

It walks on the tops of the trees and ripples waves on the lochs,

Turn your heads upward and open your eyes — I am here!

HP: Sea-Lighting the Sea Candle

I am the sea, which surrounds this Island, the water, which fills the lochs,

It is into me that .... veins flow!

Listen to my waves as they tumble over the shore.

I will gather the rain from the sky and it is into my lap that your tears fall.

I will wash you clean and carry you to distant shores.

Feel safe for I surround you!

HPS: Call to Goddess

............, I bid you Hail and Welcome!

All: Hail and Welcome!

HP: Call to God

............, I bid you Hail and Welcome!

All: Hail and Welcome!

Call to the Spirit of this place

(This can be read by one of the sponsors, or can be said by the HPS.)

Call to the Ancestors

I call to my ancestors, those of my family and friends who have gone on to the Summerlands.

To my family clan of .... those of my bloodline, to the .... family, to which I belong by marriage and by choice. And lastly, I call to the ancestors who lived and worked in this special place, those whose feet stood on the same ground I stand on today and I ask you to be with me now and watch over this ceremony, I bid you Hail and Welcome!

All: Hail and Welcome.

Reading: A short reading from............ will be read by ....

HPS: About this Handfasting

Dear friends, we have gathered together in this sacred place to celebrate the marriage between .... and ...., Such a marriage transcends any purely legal commitment made before a representative of the State, because it is celebrated before the Deities, and our ancestors thus cannot be entered into lightly or set aside with impunity. Since ancient times, marriage has been a custom wherein a man and a woman are joined together for mutual support, love and care, and if so desired there union can be blessed and enriched with children.

HP: Can I ask .... to come and light their Handfasting Candle. And can I ask everyone to join in with the words of the candle blessing.

Candle Lighting

All:
Peace of the running water to you,
Peace of the flowing air to you,
Peace of the quiet earth to you,
Peace of the shining stars to you,
And the love and care of all of us here!

Music: A piece of music/song will be played/sung by ....

The Handfasting

HPS: *(Bride and Groom),* can I ask you to turn to face each other now as we begin the main part of this Handfasting ceremony.

HPS: *(Groom)* ...., please turn to face your bride and listen to my words:
   (steps up to the bridegroom and reads...)
   O man, behold thy chosen woman and gaze upon her beauty.

Thou must know that she is made in the image of the Goddess, glorious and beautiful, strong and wise, priestess and mother. See in her thy fulfillment in love and companionship. See in her thy inner feminine self and rejoice that in her thou mayest find fulfillment. See in her womanhood the grail of immortality, the sacred cauldron that is the very cradle of life itself.

HP: *(Steps up to the Bride and reads…)*
O woman, behold thy chosen man and gaze upon his beauty. Thou must know that he is made in the image of the God, strong and upright, the protector of the weak, who shall be thy loyal soul mate. See in his manhood the sword of power from which flows the very force that gives us life. Rejoice in the strength of his embrace and be whole!

Blessing of the Rings and Legal Declaration

(HP will ask for the rings at this point)

HP: A ring is a symbol of eternity, of the continuing cycle of birth, death and rebirth. It's also a circle of protection that one person wishes to give to another, in this case ………… *(holding the two rings in his hand, the words of this will change, but the basic meaning will be the same)*

HPS: *(Placing her hand over the top of the rings in the HP's hand)* We ask a blessing on these rings and consecrate them in the names of *(Goddess and God)*

HP: *(Bride)*…………, can I now ask you to read your vows to your future husband:

Bride: *Reads her vows which will include the legal declaration:*

HPS: *(Groom)* ...., can I now ask you to read your vows to your future wife,

Groom: *(Reads his vows to his Bride which will include the legal declaration)*

The Celebrants and one other person, possibly one of the guests, steps forward and takes each cord in turn. Colors for Goddess, God and the Earth.

HP: May the God and the Sun bear witness that these two persons wish to be joined together.

HPS: May the Goddess and the Moon bear witness that these two persons wish to be joined together.

Third Persons: May the the Earth our Mother, and all here present bear witness that these two persons wish to be joined together.

HPS: I now declare that you are husband and wife!

(The couple lift their bound hands up so all can see, turning around to face everyone present.)

All: *(Clapping and cheers, couple then hug/kiss)*
The Sacred Meal

(The Celebrants Bless and consecrate the mead and bread, they then offer it first to the Bride and Groom, they offer a toast as normal, suitable for the occasion. Two helpers step forward to assist and start to take the mead and bread round the circle, in a clockwise direction giving assistance if needed to all our guests. Each person has time to offer a toast to anyone or anything they wish, as normal.)
　　*Libation to the Gods while this is taking place!

At this point if there are drums or other musical instruments, these can be used to ask the spirit to flow amongst us all!

HP: Handfasting Blessing

Now you will feel no rain,
For each will shelter the other.
Now you will feel no cold,
For each will warm the other.
Now you will feel no solitude,
For each will company the other.
Now you are two persons,
But both will lead one life.
Go now to your dwelling place,
To begin the days of your life together,
And may your days be good and long upon the Earth.
And in another time and place,
May you meet again, know and love again,
Throughout Eternity.

HPS: It's now come to the time to say goodbye to all we have asked to be with us, we will do this starting with the last person to be called.

The Closing Ceremony

Farewell to Ancestors:

Ancestors of my blood, my line, I thank you for being with us here today and witnessing our Handfasting, with love in our hearts I bid you Farewell!

All: Hail and Farewell!

Farewell to Spirit of Place!

All: Hail and Farewell!

Farewell to the God!

All: Hail and Farewell!

Farewell to the Goddess!

All: Hail and Farewell!

Farewell to the Elements!

All: Hail and Farewell!

HP: Farewell to the Sea
I am the sea, which surrounds this Island,
    I have washed you clean and I have caught your tears as they fell
into my lap,
    remember that I surround you and you are safe!
    I bless you now, Farewell!

All: Hail and Farewell!

HPS: Farewell to the Sky
I am above and around your head and my breath fills your lungs,
    Remember this gentle breeze that brings fresh air to this place!
    Turn your heads upwards and look at this Sky,
    I bless you now, Farewell!

All: Hail and Farewell!

HP: Farewell to the Earth.

I am that solid ground, which supports you,

The brown mud, which holds the roots of all plants,
With your bare feet, feel me, link with me!
I bless you now, Farewell!

All: Hail and Farewell!

Opening the Circle

(While the HPS takes a wand, the HP will read from a card the prayer for the opening of the circle, once this is done and the candles have been blown out, the spiritual part of the wedding ceremony has ended and the register will be signed and photos taken.)

(HP blows out the Handfasting candle, and the three votive candle holders will please blow out their candles)

This short ceremony was written for a couple who were not able to obtain all their paperwork in time for the major wedding they had organized and paid for. Under the circumstances, we would go ahead with a non-legal Handfasting with all the trimmings and the couple would then have all their wedding photos taken and go on to their reception. Many of the guests would not be any the wiser that there had been any problem at all. Then just as soon as the paperwork could be obtained and booked this little ceremony can go ahead.

The ceremony may also be useful for a couple who have been together for many years and do not want to have a full-blown Wedding but still need to have a Pagan Legal Ceremony.

The Ceremony actually only takes about ten minutes and then a couple of extra minutes to sign the paperwork.

A Short, Simple, Legal Pagan Handfasting

Abbreviations:

C1 — Main Legal Celebrant

C2 — Celebrant

C2: Let there be Peace throughout the World! *(The Celebrant may bang their staff on the ground or simply stamp the ground)*

C1: Let Peace surround us, and as we quiet our minds, and as we do this, we ask the elements of Air, Fire, Water, Earth and Spirit to be with us and lend us their power.

C2: Ancestors of our line, of blood and of this place, we welcome you along to witness this short ceremony.

C2: Mother Earth, Father Sky, we call to you and ask that you also stand with us as we complete this marriage ceremony.

C1: Dear Friends, we have gathered together in this special place to complete the marriage of *John* and *Jane*. Such a marriage transcends any purely legal commitment made before a representative of the state, because it is celebrated before Deities and our Ancestors thus cannot be entered into lightly or set aside with impunity. Since ancient times, marriage has been a custom wherein a man and a woman are joined together for mutual support, love and care.

C2: Can I now ask you both to read your vows to each other. *(Bride) Jane* first.

Bride's Vows:

I, ... (full name),

    Declare that I take you, ... (full name)

    to be my lawful Husband.

    You are the one I have chosen to spend the rest of my life with,

    I love and trust you without question.

    You are the one I want to see when I first open my eyes from sleep,

    And it is you that I want to give my last kiss to before I fall asleep.

I am the one who will support and protect you.

I will be there for you, whenever you need me.

As the Sun lights each day, and the Moon lights the night,

I will be there for you throughout our Springs, Summers, Autumns and Winters.

And death shall not part us;

for in the fullness of time, once more we shall find each other;

and will know, and remember, to love again, throughout eternity.

C1: *(Groom) John* will you please read your vows now?

I, ... (full name) declare that I take you, ...(Full name),

to be my lawful Wife.

You are the one I have chosen to spend the rest of my life with,

I love and trust you without question.

You are the one I want to see when I first open my eyes from sleep,

And it is you that I want to give my last kiss to before I fall asleep.

I am the one who will support and protect you.

I will be there for you, whenever you need me.

As the Sun lights each day, and the Moon lights the night,

I will be there for you throughout our Springs, Summers, Autumns and Winters.

And death shall not part us;

for in the fullness of time, once more we shall find each other;

and will know, and remember, to love again, throughout eternity.

C2: Will you please turn and face each other while we wind the Handfasting cord around your wrists.

C2: May Father Sky bear witness that these two persons wish to be joined to each other.

C1: May Mother Earth bear witness that these two persons which to be joined to each other.

Witness: May the Earth our Mother and all here present bear witness that these two persons wish to be joined to each other.

C1: .... and ...., I now declare you Husband and Wife! ...., you may kiss your wife!

C2: Let us now conclude this legal ceremony by listening to the words of the Marriage Blessing...

C2: Now you will feel no rain,
For each will shelter the other.
Now you will feel no cold,
For each will warm the other.
Now you will feel no solitude
For each will company the other.
Now you are two persons,
But both will lead one life.
Go now to your dwelling place
To begin the days of your life together,
And may your days be good
And long upon the Earth.

C1: Let us thank the elements, our ancestors and our Deities for their presence here with us today and as we depart and go out into the mundane World, let us take the peace and love of all here, seen and unseen away with us.

C2: This ceremony ends in Peace as in Peace it began, so mote it be!

All: So mote it be!

Rite of Passing and Burial

Those of you who are practicing Pagan or Heathen will understand that this is for all of us a bittersweet time. While we are happy that our loved one has passed on to the Summerlands, we are also very sad ourselves for our own loss. None of us would want anyone to suffer, and it is to be hoped that any suffering that we could see .... (name) had has now passed.

We believe that a person is made up of three parts, body, soul and spirit. At birth, all three of these things join together and stay within that body for its time on this plane of existence. At death, the body separates from the soul and spirit and the two latter parts move off.

The body is the physical skin and bone, the cells which have life in each one of them, the soul are the memories and the personality and the spirit is the energy spark, that natural electricity that fires all three and makes us whole. We understand that at death these last two move on, away to join our ancestors and rests in their halls until healing has taken place.

We understand that this life is not all there is, we know and we have faith to understand that there is another life after this, one that is fast and quick. One that vibrates at a very high rate, too fast for most of us to see or feel. Yet there are times when we feel the presence of our loved ones near us, we know they visit and at times, they even leave us a sign, move a painting or a photo perhaps.

So in the knowledge that our dear .... (name) is here with us, we will speak to him/her and let him/her know that we are going to perform this last ritual for them and with respect, bury their earthly remains and give them back to Mother Earth.

Pagan Druidcraft Burial Ceremony

First, we are going to ask some of .... (name) friends and family to call to the four elements, in the same way that we know that they would wish them to be called, so starting in the North and moving around the circle in an anticlockwise direction we will call to the elements, the directions and to the creatures most associated with these.

North: We call to the Earth in the North, to the great bear of the starry heavens to the deep dark caves and the solid ground on which .... (name) stood his/her life. We ask you to be with us all now and we bid you Hail and Welcome!

All: Hail and Welcome!

West: We call to the Water in the West, to the Salmon of wisdom that swims in the rivers and lochs, to the depth of emotion for which .... (name) had so much and we ask that you join us here for this ceremony, we bid you Hail and Welcome!

All: Hail and Welcome!

South: We call to the Fire in the South, to the great Stag in the heat of the chase, to the passion and energy that .... (name) showed in his/her life and we ask you to join us now, we bid you Hail and Welcome!

All: Hail and Welcome!

East: We call to the Air in the East, to the hawk who circles in the clear blue sky, to the quickness of thought and of movement that .... (name) in his/her lifetime was known for. We ask you to be with us now and we bid you Hail and Welcome!

All: Hail and Welcome!

A Call to the Spirit of Place, the Guardian of this Place:
Guardian spirit of this beautiful place, patron Deity who lives in this area, we call to you, we are sad for ourselves and yet glad for .... (name). We mean you no harm and we call with respect to you and ask you to join us now, watch over us as we conduct this last rite for .... (name). Welcome amongst us guardian spirit, we bid you Hail and Welcome!

All: Hail and Welcome!

A Call to .... (name) Ancestors: We call to the ancestors of .... (name), of his/her line, blood and of this place. We know you are very close today, as you have been over the last few days and we ask you now to take care of our dear .... (name), lead him/her gently into the new life in the Summerlands. Come join us now and celebrate with us, Hail and Welcome!

All: Hail and welcome!

A Call to the Dark God:
We call to the Gatherer of Souls, the Horned God who waits at the Gates of Death. We know you as Herne, Cernunnos and Hades, heed our calls, you who are the consort and mate of the Mother Goddess, we ask you to speak to us at the Dark Moon when all is still and awaiting new birth.

I am he who stands at the gates of death, you know me as wild and free,
    I am the fire of your soul and the hunter of knowledge.
    My mate and consort is all to me and to you,
    Like her, I am strong and young, wild and free,
    You know me as lover and friend, as father and brother,
    But it is me that welds the scythe of time and I stand in the midnight stillness, in the small hours when life and death stand

side by side.

So come to me, you are my children and I am your father,
  I am the passion and the seed,
  I am the fire, the strength and the blade,
  I will give you peace through love and death,
  Take my hand and together we will stand and guard she who sleeps in the depths of the earth.

A Call to the Dark Goddess:

We Call to the Dark Goddess, she who is known as Cerridwen, Hekate, Morgaine, and by other fearful names.

She is the Dark Mother of all creation, it is she who calls to us at the Dark of the Moon and she who calls at the end of our days.

She is in the depths of the seas and the deepest darkest earth; to her we go for rest and comfort.

She too is the weaver, and is ever adjusting the web of fate.

Come then Mother of Darkness, come from behind and beneath the shadows.

I am the cold clear dark of midnight; it is to me that you come in the small hours of your existence.

I am the one who weaves the silver web, and it is I who hold the thread, which will bring you to life again.

Walk to me through the mists of time, for it is I who will always be there waiting for you.

You have known me as Maiden, in the fresh flush of your youth,

You have known me as Lover and as Mother in my fullness of maturity,

Now do you see me as Crone, Dark Hag, waiting at your day's end.

But know you, that it is also me who is the midwife of babies and of souls,

For to die is to live and without death there would be no new life.

So grieve not for your youth, you wise women and men,

Grieve not for your family and friends, for I am the promise of all new things.

Turn now to see me as Dark and Silver,

For I am the Mother into whose arms you come and I will comfort you and lead you to new things.

(Perhaps a song here)

The Burial

Celebrant: *(Please take the cords you were given for this ceremony and stand around the grave, the undertakers will assist us with this task.)*

Dark Mother, Dark Lord, we give back to you the earthly remains of our dear .... (name), he/she came from the magical creation of your energy, stayed with us for (age) years and has now moved on. We now trust her earthly remains into your safekeeping, so mote it be!

(As this prayer is said, the coffin is lowered into the grave with the help of the undertakers)

All: So mote it be!

Celebrant: Can we now ask that those of you who wish to put a little earth into the grave make that token gesture now and after the ceremony has ended, we will fill this grave with earth.

(Allow a little time for friends and family to sprinkle a little earth into the grave and while this is done a song can be sung or some gentle music played.)

(Poetry for the Departed)

Farewell to the Dark Goddess:

Dark Mother, Goddess of all creation, from the dark of the Moon and the hidden depths of our minds we call and give our thanks to you. Continue to watch over us as we leave this place and make our journey home. Thank you for the love you have always shown .... (name) and ourselves, now go if you must but stay if you will, we bid you Hail and Farewell!

All: Hail and Farewell!

Farewell to the Dark God:
Dark Father, God of creation who with the Mother Goddess gives life to all, from the stillness of the night we call and give our thanks to you for the love and protection you have always shown .... (name). Now stay with us and watch over us as we make our way back to our own homes. Thank you for being here with us and we bid you Hail and Farewell!

All: Hail and Farewell!

A Word to the Ancestors:
Ancestors of our line, blood and place, we are so very aware of your presence with us today and we thank you for this. Continue to help (name) in their new life in the Summerlands and watch over us in the days to come. We bid you Hail and Farewell!

All: Hail and Farewell!

Thanks to the Spirit of Place:
Spirit of this beautiful place, of the valleys and fields around us, of its rivers and lochs, you who watches over this very special place, thank you for being with us here today, now go if you must but stay if you can, I bid you Hail and Farewell!

All: Hail and Farewell!

East: We call with thanks to the Air in the East, to the Hawk circling in the clear blue sky. We are grateful for the quickness of thought you have brought to this ceremony, we bid you Hail and Farewell!

All: Hail and Farewell!

South: We call with thanks to the Fire in the South and to the great Stag whose energy, passion and love fills our lives. We have been aware of your presence today and we bid you Hail and Farewell!

All: Hail and Farewell!

West: We call with thanks to the Water in the West and to the Salmon of wisdom who swims in our waters. For the emotion and empathy you have given us today we thank you and we bid you Hail and Farewell.

All: Hail and Farewell!

North: We call with thanks to the Earth in the North, to the great bear of the starry heavens and the deep abiding ground. We are grateful for your stability and protection you have given us today, and we bid you Hail and Farewell!

All: Hail and Farewell!

Before we all leave this place it is now our task to help fill the earth into this hole that we have lowered .... (name) into, so will those of you who feel able, add some soil into the hole.

If you don't feel able to do this, please understand that we are all different and not all of us can cope with these things, you should only do this if you feel comfortable with this.

Blessing:
May the Peace that surrounds us here today and the energy we

have created together stay close with us as we join together in a drink and refreshments after this ceremony.

Let there be peace all over the World, in the East, South, West and North and may the energy and love of our ancestors, family and friends surround us.

We ask a blessing on .... (name) in their new life, take our love with you, and visit us in circle especially when we call on you at the times when the veil is very thin.

This Circle is open to the apparent world, merry meet, merry part and merry meet again!

A Rite of Passing Suitable for a Cremation

(Entry Music)

HP: Let us begin by asking the powers of the Elements, of Earth, Air, Fire, Water and of Spirit, to be with us today in this ceremony.

HPS: Let honor be given to the Spirit of Place that holds us here today. Let honor be given to our ancestors without whom we would not be, and in whose company .... (name) now stands. Let honor be given to the God and Goddess of this Land, may they support us in this our time of need. May we all be richer for having come here to celebrate the life of .... (name).

First Reading — *(A poem or a piece from a book perhaps.)*

HP: We stand at a gateway now, a gateway that each of us must step through at some time in our lives .... (name) has stepped through this gateway already. His/Her soul has travelled on before us to the peace and beauty of the Summerlands. The sadness and pain that we feel now is in our knowledge and our experience of the fact that we ourselves cannot yet cross that threshold to be with her until our time has come. Wherever he/she may be, and on whatever plane, let her be blessed with rest and an utter cessation from strife.

Celebration of Life

HP: Physical death is for the person experiencing it, a birth, a freeing of the self from the limitations of the body so that the soul can grow and learn and move in a brighter world. .... (name) is in this brighter world now and it is time for us to give thanks for his/her time on earth, for the joy, laughter, love and wisdom which he/she experienced and which he/she gave.

Second Reading — Ancient Spirit, written by Insa Thierling *(Can be found on the internet)*

HPS: Let us now have a moment of silence in which we each, in our own way, give thanks to .... (name) for all that he/she gave us, send .... (name) our own blessings for a safe and joyous life in the Other World — filled with peace and clarity and love.

(A few moments of silence)

HPS: As the Sun rises in the East and sets in the West, so too are each of us born and so too do each of us die. But as the Sun returns anew each day, so too do we return to Earth, refreshed and renewed. Now, ... (name) go safely, go well, go surely. Our hearts are with you. And you remain in our hearts.

HP: May the road rise up to meet you,
May the wind be always at your back,
May the sun shine warm upon your face
And the rains fall gently upon your fields.
And until we meet again
May your Gods hold you in the palms of their hands.

(Committal music)

HPS: Journey on now, brother/sister. We will follow when our time comes. May you be born again at the same time, and in the same place as those you knew and loved in this life.

HPS: Let us give thanks to the Spirit of Place that has held us here today, to our ancestors without whom we would not be standing here and in whose company .... (name) now stands.
Let us give thanks to the God and Goddess of this Land, may they continue to support us in our need as we go about our lives. May our hearts and minds hold what we have shared here today.

HP: Let us give thanks to the Elements of Earth, Air, Fire, Water and of Spirit. In Peace, we began so let us end in Peace and carry our Peace into the World.

(Closing Music)

A Passing Rite for a Much Loved Pet

I think this basic outline can be used for any pet, for sprinkling the ashes or for a pet burial. It could in fact be re-written to be used for a human's ashes as well. It is hoped that this will give you an outline that you can adapt and use.

Mother Earth, Father Sky, we ask for your blessing on this our ceremony of thanksgiving, honoring and blessing our pet .... (name) who has left this World.

Turn to face the North:
We stand at the threshold that all of us must stand when our own time comes.
Our sadness and pain comes from the fact that our dear pet has already passed this point and is no longer with us.

A word about .... (name): *(This is where you can talk about your pet, how you felt about him/her, any memories that you would like to share.)*

.... (name) put his/her trust in us to do what was best always. His/her companionship we took for granted but now that he/she has passed on, we feel the emptiness that is left.

Let us have a moment of quiet in which we each, in our own way, can give thanks to .... (name) for all that he/she gave us.

(Pause)

Mother Earth, Father Sky, we give thanks for what is given, we give thanks for what is taken.

(As the ashes are scattered)

Passing Prayer from the Celtic Devotional by Caitlin Matthews
You have been called from the place of your dwelling,
May blessed soul-friends guide you,
May helping spirits lead you,
May the Gatherer of Souls call you,
May the homeward path rise up under your feet
And lead you gladly home.

.... (name), may your journey to the Summerlands be swift and sure. We ask that the blessing of the Spirits of the Ancestors, of Time, Blood and of Place, be with you.

We ask that the powers of the Spirits of North and South, East and West bless you and be with you.

We ask for the blessing of the Lord and Lady of the Animals and the Woods, the Mountains and the Streams.

We ask that the flow of the Awen be always around you in the Summerlands.

With a blessing of the forests and streams, the mountains and the valleys be with you and also with us.

As the sun rises in the East and sets in the West, so too are each of us born and so too do each of us die. But as the sun returns anew each day, so too do we return to earth, refreshed and renewed. Dear .... (name) know that just as you have been born into the spiritual world, so too will you be born again on earth — when it is right, in your own time. Now go safely, go well, go surely. Our hearts are with you. There is no separation.

Go with our love .... (name)

So mote it be!

Personal Spiritual Steps and Development

You could ask, where do I go from here? And it's a very valid question, how many of us have taken any personal steps to deepen our spiritual lives over the last few years? No doubt all of us are guilty at some time of putting spiritual things to one side and concentrating on day to day matters, work, shopping for food and necessities, cleaning your home and relaxing. All very important to all of us so why bother with the spiritual at all?

It has been found by medical researchers that those of us who have a faith and have some form of practice and happier than those who do not believe anything spiritual. We tend to be healthier, sleep better and when we fall in love, do so with great depth of feeling. I am sure it's not a good idea to generalize in these matters, but it's certainly a very good idea to see how much of a difference putting the 'spiritual' back into our lives would make.

There are many books written about keeping a journal, writing down your experiences, keeping a dream diary and things like this. It is well known that many Pagan and Heathen folk will keep note of some of the rituals they perform and some of the magical work, with a note on how it all went and the result if any of this.

But on a personal level how can we tune in a little better?

If you are not a member of a group of some kind, if you are not trained in any particular path, and you want to make your day to day experience a little deeper I can offer a few little tips, very simple ones.

I'm a great researcher into family history and the reason is this, if you know who your ancestors were then you can picture them in your mind, what they may have done, how they worked all of this brings you closer to getting to know yourself. So if you have not done so already, find out a little about your ancestors and the next time you call to them, picture them in your mind, speak directly to them.

Greet each day as it comes; acknowledge that you live on this Earth, if it's sunny then send some positive thanks in your mind to the Solar Deity for their kindness in warming and lightening your day. If it's raining, then a thought to the Deity of our rivers and lakes, of wells and the sea surrounding us, remember that we do need this rain for without it our trees would not flourish, they would not have green leaves which help us to breathe. So give thanks for enough rain and perhaps also make a point of asking for just enough!

Tune into the ever-changing seasons and try to feel the difference as the wheel turns.

If, after a while, maybe a few months you have been doing some basic things like this and you want to try more, then maybe put aside a few moments from time to time, light a candle, watch the flame and meditate on the life within all of nature. Be still and listen, shut the day to day noise out and listen to what your inner voice tells you, or maybe a guardian spirit will speak to you. If you are never still, never listen, how can you ever hear?

Plan to celebrate the different ceremonies for the wheel of the year, use these rituals and alter them a little to suit your own surroundings. Speak to a few of your friends and perhaps agree to meet together and hold a ceremony, then maybe go for tea or coffee afterwards or if you are able to get to the shore, and the weather is warm enough, perhaps a picnic is possible.

If you start to do all of these little steps and you still want more you might think about some kind of training. You may be drawn to Druidry or perhaps to Wicca. Or you may want to study Druidcraft. Or you feel drawn to a Shamanic path and you need a teacher, all of these are possible. It just may take a while before you find the right person.

Some time ago, I wrote a little ceremony for a dedication into Druidcraft, but not one person has ever asked me to help them dedicate themselves, so perhaps this is something you would want to do on your own and in private.

Further Development

If you are lucky enough to live near Glasgow in Scotland or you can plan a holiday so that you could visit at some stage, or if you are interested in connecting with others of like mind. Tuatha de Bridget does now have a study course, which runs over thirteen months, there are four face to face meetings each year and it's very much up to you how much you put into the course. We have mentors and each student is allocated a mentor. How much does all this cost? The answer is your time and effort, and a £1 coin to put into the kitty for any face-to-face meetings or indeed if you make it along to any of the festival ceremonies. You would need to be online, and be able to do the research and work yourself. The course is called 'The Way Forward' and we have students in other parts of the world and I hope in time they might be able to run the course in their home country and widen the teaching.

For spiritual development, you really need to meet up with your friends in your small group at least once a month, more often if possible and learn to meditate, to breathe and relax and to share with each other your experiences. One of you would need to host the meeting and agree to bring folks back to the here and now from a meditation, and if you raise any energy in your meetings, the best place to send it is out into the world for healing.

If you feel I or my group can help you with your development, or you simply want to tell us about your experience with the rituals in this book, then write to me using the contact details given with this book.

Let the Spirit of Inspiration and love fill your mind and heart, bubble over into your day-to-day life and bring you peace.

So Mote it Be!

Siusaidh Ceanadach, Glasgow, Scotland, 2011.

Appendix

Yule Incense Recipe

Ingredients

2 parts of Frankincense
2 parts of Scots Pine, Colophony.
1 part of Sandalwood
1 part of Juniper berries
1 part of dried orange rind
2 parts of Oak Bark
½ part of cloves
10 drops of Vertivert essential oil
9 drops of Rose Geranium

Method

Put the resin granules, the frankincense and pine into a pestle and mortar and grind together, leave plenty of larger pieces. Add all the dry ingredients and mix with the resin with a metal spoon.

Lastly add the pure essential oils and mix again with a metal spoon.

Put the mix into little glass jars and seal with a lid, leave to mature for about a month at least.

Tip: Use only glass or china bowls and use a metal spoon, anything plastic will absorb the oils and gum and could not be used for anything else afterwards.

About the Author

Siusaidh Ceanadach has been Pagan for over twenty five years. She trained as an Astrologer in London and became a Wiccan, training in an Alexandrian Coven. Since then she has studied Druidry with The Order of Bards, Ovates and Druids and with The Druid Network. Her life took her to live in Scotland where she became elevated into Gardnerian Wicca and has since, along with her husband and High Priest has run a Coven, a Development Circle and co-ordinates The Tuatha De Bridget, open Druidcraft Groven in Glasgow, Scotland, UK.

Siusaidh is a recognised Legal Celebrant with The Pagan Federation in Scotland and conducts Handfastings, Baby Naming and Funeral Ceremonies. She has a wide circle of friends Worldwide and is well known in Wiccan and Pagan circles.

Siusaidh can be found easily online via email, via Facebook, and through Siusaidh and Piet's site: www.paganhandfast ingscotland.co.uk

Moon Books invites you to begin or deepen your encounter with Paganism, in all its rich, creative, flourishing forms.